More Advance Praise for
A MAD LOVE

"Opera composers often spin out just a thought or two into expansive arias. Vivien Schweitzer does the opposite, deftly packing centuries of music and a profusion of astute observations into this lean delight of a book. If you think you might like opera, but have no idea where to start, the answer is: right here."

> —Justin Davidson, Pulitzer Prize–winning classical music critic, *New York Magazine*

"A lively and engaging introduction to an art form that belongs to us all, whether or not we know it yet. Welcome in."

> —Tim Page, Pulitzer Prize–winning critic and professor of music and journalism, University of Southern California

A MAD LOVE

A MAD LOVE

AN INTRODUCTION TO OPERA

VIVIEN SCHWEITZER

BASIC BOOKS
New York

Basic Books
Hachette Book Group
1290 Avenue of the Americas, New York, NY 10104
www.basicbooks.com

Printed in the United States of America

First Edition: September 2018

Published by Basic Books, an imprint of Perseus Books, LLC, a subsidiary of Hachette Book Group, Inc. The Basic Books name and logo is a trademark of the Hachette Book Group.

The Hachette Speakers Bureau provides a wide range of authors for speaking events. To find out more, go to www.hachettespeakersbureau.com or call (866) 376-6591.

The publisher is not responsible for websites (or their content) that are not owned by the publisher.

Print book interior design by Amy Quinn.

The Library of Congress has cataloged the hardcover edition as follows:
Names: Schweitzer, Vivien, author.
Title: A mad love : an introduction to opera / Vivien Schweitzer.
Description: First edition. | New York : Basic Books, 2018. | Includes bibliographical references and index.
Identifiers: LCCN 2018008455 (print) | LCCN 2018009702 (ebook) | ISBN 9780465096947 (ebook) | ISBN 9780465096930 (hardcover)
Subjects: LCSH: Opera.
Classification: LCC ML1700 (ebook) | LCC ML1700 .S395 2018 (print) | DDC 782.1—dc23
LC record available at https:lccn.loc.gov/2018008455

ISBNs: 978-0-465-09693-0 (hardcover), 978-0-465-09694-7 (ebook)

LSC-C

10 9 8 7 6 5 4 3 2 1

For my uncle, Richard Field

CONTENTS

PREFACE

As I scanned the opera news alerts in my inbox recently an unusual headline caught my eye: "Chamber Pot Opera's Queen Victoria Building Venue an Inconvenience for Some." The article, from the June 4, 2017, *Sydney Morning Herald*, discussed the "unusual challenges" of staging opera in a public restroom. Opera in the bathroom? This site-specific venture perhaps took the idea of singing in the shower a bit too far, but it demonstrated how the art form is evolving in the twenty-first century: opera today is both surprising and thriving. In recent years, in New York alone, I've attended performances staged in a former bus depot in an industrial part of Brooklyn, listened to members of an opera collective perform in subway stations, attended live broadcasts in movie theaters, and watched an outdoor screening of Verdi's *La traviata* at Lincoln Center Plaza, a performance that held a huge and diverse crowd spellbound. And, of course, I've attended performances in traditional theaters to enjoy the unamplified voices of world-class singers—the most visceral thrill of opera. It seems there have never been more ways to experience opera, whether under the stars, under the chandeliers, or possibly, even, in a powder room near you.

Throughout history people have sung to express joy and sadness, and in opera, those emotions are magnified: live opera is a shared event that can be profoundly cathartic. It's often noted that opera, with its fantastical stories, requires a suspension of disbelief. The audience must accept that a heroine can sing passionately while dying of tuberculosis, or that people can fall in love a millisecond after meeting. As demonstrated by the success of *Harry Potter*, *Star Wars*, and *Wonder Woman*, however, contemporary audiences seem to have a healthy capacity to enjoy the unreal. In opera, no matter how unlikely a situation or fantastical a character, he or she represents very human frailties, desires, and emotions. The sorceress Alcina in Handel's opera of the same name may perform impossible feats of magic, but this does not negate the truth of her emotions. Perhaps the only truly surreal aspect of opera is that an unamplified human voice can fill a large theater with an intensity that seems to have been conjured by a magician's wand. I've been deeply moved while listening to Joyce DiDonato convey the despair of one of Handel's heroines, and thrilled by Nina Stemme's hair-raising portrayal of the insane Elektra. I've been awestruck by the virtuosity of the tenors Lawrence Brownlee and Javier Camarena, and by the way Vittorio Grigolo's radiant voice so easily fills the cavernous space of the Metropolitan Opera House.

Opera buffs have long been a nostalgic bunch, although a character in a play by the British polymath Noël Coward observes that "people are wrong when they say opera is not what it used to be. It is what it used to be. That is what's wrong with it." Or perhaps that's what's right with it. It's a golden age for opera, and whatever the indisputable glories of the past, there are many fantastic artists who are both superb singers and much better actors than their predecessors. The abundance of talent doesn't diminish the significant financial difficulties facing opera institutions of all sizes. Glass-half-empty observers have also noted the paucity of new works receiving premieres compared to past eras. But from a more optimistic perspective, it's an exciting time, not only because of the gifted singing actors working today, but also because of the sheer diversity of repertory being presented. By the late twentieth century, the beauty of long-neglected operas by composers such as Monteverdi and Handel had been revealed by insightful scholars and musicians, and invariably there's an energetic artist or musicologist dusting off another obscure corner of the repertory for our enjoyment. In recent years there has also been a proliferation of small, adventurous opera companies offering high-quality productions and first-rate young singers. And although most composers aren't churning out dozens of operas like some of their predecessors, despite the enormous creative and financial challenges of creating opera in the twenty-first century there have been some terrific recent works on topical subjects such as gay rights, terrorism, and the death penalty.

In order to fully appreciate operas by living composers, it's essential to understand the four-hundred-year tradition behind them. Opera has been the entertainment of both the one percent and the masses, and the pendulum has swung both ways. Composers, musicians, academics, and moralists have debated whether opera should instruct, entertain, or move listeners, and just how it should go about doing so. Generations of composers have been criticized, censored, and feted—and sometimes all of the above—for their musical depictions of love, madness, and death. Though no experience is necessary to admire the operatic voice or enjoy a popular opera like *Carmen*, to engage with opera on a deeper level and fully appreciate what you're seeing and hearing, it's vital to understand opera's history, styles, and performance traditions.

I wrote my first (unpublished) opera review at age fifteen, after seeing a performance of Strauss's *Arabella* at the Royal Opera House in London, with the soprano Kiri Te Kanawa in the title role. I recently rediscovered this youthful assessment, in which I described Te Kanawa as "magnificent" and the orchestra "excellent," albeit "occasionally a tad loud because I couldn't hear the singers." I was also impressed with the singer performing the role of Arabella's brother, who, I noted in the review, "is really a girl." I wasn't then familiar with the gender-bending elements inherent to much opera, or with the concept of a "trouser role," in which women sing the roles of young men.

If you simply want to know the definitions of opera terminology—such as trouser role, or opera seria, or coloratura—the answers are of course only a Google search away. Instead of offering a comprehensive survey of operas or complete, detailed synopses, I have aimed to embed the fundamentals of the Western operatic tradition in a narrative context to show how composers have used different techniques and voices to create sung drama. To understand why it's a strange directorial choice in the twenty-first century to cast a baritone as Handel's Giulio Cesare, for example, you need to know about the evolution and categorization of voice types. To appreciate how a director's staging of *Carmen* deviates from tradition, it helps to be aware of how the opera has typically been staged. To comprehend why the pianist and composer Clara Schumann called Wagner's *Tristan and Isolde* "disgusting," and why the opera was so shocking to listeners, you need to explore Wagner's radical musical ideas. And to see why some detractors claimed that the composer John Adams "humanized" terrorists in his controversial opera *The Death of Klinghoffer*, it's useful to examine how he used music to tell this particular story.

I reviewed opera and classical music for the *New York Times* between 2006 and 2016 and interviewed some of the genre's finest practitioners: the singers, composers, conductors, and directors who make it happen. That experience of listening to and critiquing opera on a regular basis informs this book, as does my own experience as a classical pianist. Pianists often try to emulate singers: to breathe at the right time so that a phrase unfolds naturally, to convey the music's emotions and narrative structure, and to make our instrument "sing." Conveying feeling is an integral part of almost all music, with or without words.

Although opera is certainly no longer the popular art form it has been in past centuries, it's also far from its elitist origins in the early seventeenth century, when it was created and performed for royalty. Antonio Pappano, music director of the Royal Opera, told *The Guardian* in 2014 that he finds the elitist label often (and unfairly) applied to opera to be "tiresome." Opera "is so visceral, so emotional—and so incredibly thrilling when it's good," he said. He's absolutely right: opera done right is an experience that has moved listeners throughout the centuries—in theaters, in parks, in bus depots, and in the royal courts where it all began.

I've created an extensive public Spotify Playlist (called *A Mad Love: An Introduction to Opera*) to accompany this book: it mirrors the chapter content and features much of the music discussed, beginning with Monteverdi's *L'Orfeo*, the first successful opera, and concluding with operas that premiered in 2017, some four hundred years later. I hope you enjoy the journey.

CHAPTER 1

FROM GODS TO MORTALS

On Monteverdi and the birth of opera,
French baroque opera, Handel, and Mozart

Orpheus, the musician and poet of Greek mythology, could tame wild animals, calm turbulent seas, and placate gods with his beautiful voice. After his bride, Eurydice, was killed by a snake, he used his talents to rescue her from the underworld. Its rulers were so touched by Orpheus's singing that they allowed the grief-stricken musician to take Eurydice back home, on one condition: he was instructed to walk in front of her on the journey from the abyss and not glance back, or he would lose her forever. Despite this ominous warning, he was unable to give her the cold shoulder and turned to face her, with tragic consequences. The myth is about human frailty—how passion can so easily override reason. But it is also about the power of a glorious voice to provoke an emotional reaction in the listener. If Orpheus had merely arrived in the underworld and said: "Hello, may I please have my wife back?" the stony-hearted gods would presumably have been much less sympathetic: it was by singing his plea that he won his case.

The opera *L'Orfeo* (*Orpheus*) by the composer Claudio Monteverdi received its premiere in 1607 at the Ducal Palace of Mantua in northern Italy. It was performed for a small aristocratic audience that would have been familiar with the Orpheus myth, which had already recently been told in other works of musical theater. According to a court theologian, "both poet and musician have depicted the inclinations of the heart so skillfully that it could not have been done better." A repeat performance was scheduled just a few days later. Music had been prominent in both secular and religious traditions in Europe long before 1600, but composers, including Monteverdi—an employee of the Court of Mantua who wrote music for religious, secular, and festive occasions, as well as music for the theater—had begun to experiment with a different way of combining music and poetry to tell a story. They were creating works in which the actors would sing their lines instead of speaking them, as was then customary in the theater. By the end of Monteverdi's lifetime, this form of sung drama had become known as *opera*. *L'Orfeo* wasn't the first opera, but it is widely acknowledged as the first successful one—a pivotal moment when music, poetry, and song were combined to tell a story in a compelling way. *L'Orfeo* certainly set a precedent for passion eclipsing reason in opera, a genre whose extravagance prompted the British statesman and writer Lord Chesterfield to write to his son, in 1752, "Whenever

I go to an opera, I leave my sense and reason at the door with my half-guinea, and deliver myself up to my eyes and my ears." As opera developed in the ensuing centuries, it often continued to be neither sensible nor reasonable, although there have been innumerable cerebral attempts to rein in its excesses. Orpheus may have subdued the beasts, but it's fortunate that no one has ever succeeded in taming opera—an exuberant, passionate, and all-encompassing art form.

Monteverdi's opera didn't emerge out of the blue, like a mythical creature rearing its head. It was the product of centuries of musical tradition in Western Europe. In the Middle Ages, secular entertainment included troubadours who sang ballads about love, and in Renaissance Italy pastoral plays (inspired by bucolic natural scenes) featured dance and song. The use of music in theater was further developed in the *intermedio*, an entertainment performed between acts of lavish, elaborately staged spectacles honoring the royal weddings of important families, such as the Medicis. On the religious front, liturgical dramas were used to spread the gospel, and singing was an important element of Roman Catholic church services. In the Middle Ages, the Mass included an unaccompanied type of singing called *plainchant*, which is *monophonic*—that is, having one melodic line sung in unison. The twelfth-century German abbess Hildegard von Bingen, whose 1098 birth was celebrated in 1998 with a spate of recordings and performances, wrote chants with soaring, melodic lines that sound both pure and rapturous. Much medieval music is anonymous: Von Bingen, who was canonized in 2012, is one of the first known composers, a notable fact, given the struggles women composers have faced gaining recognition over the centuries. She experienced visions—possibly migraine-induced hallucinations—and became a remarkable polymath, writing a morality play as well as scholarly texts about botany, theology, and medicine; she also founded a monastery and corresponded with heads of state and religious authorities.

When church singing was monophonic, the text could be easily understood by parishioners, but by the Renaissance music had become *polyphonic*, meaning that different melodies were sung simultaneously. Although polyphonic music can sound glorious, the overlapping melodic lines often render the text unintelligible to the listener, just as the images in a stained-glass window can become blurred when sunlight pours through the panes of glass. Renaissance church officials fretted that the music was becoming so elaborate that congregants couldn't understand the words. In their minds, this was problematic: they wanted their parishioners to imbibe the gospel through music, not swoon in the pews over the beauty of the harmonies. The difficulty of deciphering text submerged by complex polyphonic lines also irked those in secular communities, albeit for more earthbound reasons. Whereas church officials wanted easily decipherable song texts to inspire parishioners to greater devotion, intellectuals like Vincenzo Galilei (father of the astronomer Galileo) wanted words to propel the drama.

Galilei was a member of the Florentine Camerata, a group of intellectuals and musicians who met regularly at the end of the sixteenth century in the palace of Count

Bardi, a Florentine patron of the arts. Members of the Camerata, who shared the fascination of many Renaissance artists with the ancient Romans and Greeks, studied the classics intensively. Music was important for the Greeks, who sang epic poetry, sometimes accompanied by the lyre. The Camerata's members examined the role of the Greek chorus (a collective moral voice commenting on the action) and the way music might have propelled the drama. Since there were no surviving documents of ancient music, they read primary sources, such as Aristotle's *Poetics*, in which he wrote that the audience watching a tragic drama would feel such empathy for the characters that the experience would be cathartic. The Camerata deemed such catharsis impossible to have been attained by merely listening to spoken text and thought that the words must have been sung. Galilei disapproved of the fact that the polyphonic music of his own era served mainly "to delight the ear, while that of ancient music is to induce in another the same passion that one feels oneself": "No person of judgment," he wrote, referring to the polyphonic style, "can understand the expression of sense and meaning through words set in this absurd manner." In 1581, Galilei collaborated with another scholar of the classics to write a treatise about creating a new genre of music that would be inspired by the Greek theatrical model—and in which the words must be intelligible.

The Renaissance composers and librettists who adopted the Camerata's ideas wrote monophonic, sparsely accompanied vocal lines and set the texts in a way that emphasized the natural rhythms of speaking. *Dafne* (*Daphne*), which has a score by Jacopo Peri and Jacopo Corsi, and was performed around 1598 in a private salon, is considered by most scholars to be the first opera, although only fragments survive. After *Dafne*, Peri wrote *Euridice* (*Eurydice*), the first complete surviving opera. It was inspired by the same myth as Monteverdi's *L'Orfeo*, but the music is far less memorable and doesn't add much emotional nuance to the story. Monteverdi's version of the legend, which premiered the same year he lost his own beloved wife, is widely considered the first successful opera because of the ingenuity of the orchestral and vocal music and the way he conveys the emotional plight of the characters.

L'Orfeo has a libretto by Alessandro Striggio, inspired by the Roman poet Ovid's *Metamorphoses*. In his version of the Orpheus myth, Ovid wrote that after hearing Orpheus sing, "for the first time, the faces of the furies were wet with tears, won over by his song: the king of the deep, and his royal bride, could not bear to refuse his prayer and called for Eurydice." Monteverdi illustrates the story and brings different emotions to the fore with various instruments, including the bright sound of trumpets and strings in the joyous fanfare that opens the opera. He uses strings, harpsichord, and recorders to convey the blissful mood of pastoral scenes; a harp to depict Orfeo's lyre; and the darker hues of trombones and cornetti to evoke Hades. (A *cornetto* is a Renaissance instrument that looks like a curved recorder with a trumpet mouthpiece.) The choir has the role of a Greek chorus and comments on the action, its upbeat, buoyant music a stark contrast to the mournful tone of the solo songs. The music of the chorus of nymphs and shepherds, who in Act I express their happiness about

Orfeo's newfound wedded bliss, contrasts with his emotive ode to his beloved Eurydice, which is infused with a gentle melancholy that foreshadows the upcoming disaster.

One of Monteverdi's many contributions to opera was the development of the *aria*—a solo song whose function in opera is to convey emotion and give characters a chance to express their feelings about a particular situation or person. Just as hearing a powerfully delivered soliloquy in a Shakespeare play might be the dramatic and emotional highlight, listening to your favorite singer perform a gorgeous aria is invariably a highlight of the opera experience. Orfeo's Act III centerpiece, "Possente spirto, e formidabil nume" (Mighty spirit and formidable God), is one of the first important arias in opera. Preceded by a mournful chorus of trombones, Orfeo's potent lament is also a plea to Charon, ferryman of the dead, to let him enter the underworld so he can rescue Eurydice. Monteverdi, as was common at the time, encouraged the singer to ornament the vocal line and provided embellished versions of such arias. The vocal lines are *melismatic*—which means that multiple pitches are sung on one syllable—a style you'll hear in music from Hildegard von Bingen to R&B. Melismas can increase the expressive impact of a particular word, as Whitney Houston did with her rendering of the word "I" in the song "I Will Always Love You." The melismatic vocal lines of "Possente spirto" convey Orfeo's emotional plight. Just as Orfeo tamed wild beasts with his voice, he lulled the boatman Charon to sleep so he could cross into Hades. In the version performed at the premiere, Orfeo (who has lost Eurydice) is eventually devoured by

Bacchus's angry maenads, who want to punish the grief-stricken musician for renouncing women and telling the shepherds to follow his example. Orfeo's rant is the first of many operatic tirades against women, but the version published a few years later ends on a less gory note: Apollo interrupts Orfeo's misogynist rant and invites him up to heaven to contemplate Eurydice's beauty.

The purpose of the aria—in which the characters reveal their emotional state—contrasts with that of the more prosaic *recitative*, which is to move the plot along. In a recitative, singers employ a more speech-like pattern; the first opera composers described it as *recitar cantando*, which translates from the Italian as "speaking in song." Another important element of Renaissance and baroque music is the *continuo*, a continuous, accompanying bass line performed on a keyboard instrument such as a harpsichord or organ, or a plucked string instrument like the harp, lute, or guitar. Just as jazz pianists have a rudimentary outline to guide their playing, the continuo player improvises on a basic line, guided by indicators as to what harmonies should be played.

Judging by eyewitness accounts of the rapturous reception given his operas, Monteverdi seems to have accomplished the Camerata's mission of providing a cathartic experience for listeners. In 1608, the audience at his second opera, *L'Arianna*, was moved to tears by the lament of the abandoned title heroine. The opera, inspired by the mythological story of Ariadne's abandonment by Theseus on the island of Naxos and her ensuing marriage to Bacchus, has a libretto based on texts by Ovid and Virgil. It was commissioned to celebrate a royal wedding in Mantua. (Only the lament survives; the rest of the opera is lost.)

L'Arianna was unusual in Monteverdi's era for the lengthy and substantive role written for a female performer (who died of smallpox during rehearsals). Women were not supposed to appear on stage with men, and in the Papal States they were legally prohibited from doing so. In this sense the nascent opera genre reflected traditions of the theater world: since women were not permitted to perform with professional theater troupes in Renaissance England, boys enacted Shakespearean roles, including Cleopatra, Juliet, and Lady Macbeth. It wasn't until more than four decades after the playwright's death in 1616 that a woman first performed one of his roles in public: Desdemona in Othello.

IN ITS EARLIEST GUISES IN ALL COUNTRIES, OPERA WAS A highly exclusive form of entertainment: it was performed in royal palaces and private salons and sponsored by and designed to flatter wealthy patrons. In Italy, rich nobles who had commissioned the intermedi for social functions, such as weddings, continued to subsidize early operas, using them as a means to flaunt their wealth, power, and taste. (In the United States, where public funding for the arts is minimal compared to Europe, wealthy patrons still subsidize opera.) By the mid-seventeenth century, opera in Venice had expanded from an elite art form to a popular one. Professionals and merchants flocked to the dozens of theaters that sprang up after the Teatro San Cassiano, the first public opera house, opened in 1637. During performances at public venues, audience members ate, drank, and flirted; those in the boxes sometimes spat on their poorer counterparts in the pit below (and engaged in other naughty behavior behind the box curtains). It wasn't until the late nineteenth century in Germany (and later in Italy) that audiences were expected to behave in a manner that contemporary listeners might consider "proper." Going to the opera used to be a rowdy affair.

Monteverdi's *L'incoronazione di Poppea* (*The Coronation of Poppea*) reflects the riotous and libertine Venetian ambience in which it was created. Lust trumps reason in this tale of passion, adultery, and ambition, which received its premiere in a public theater during Venice's Carnival season, which ends at the beginning of Lent, forty days before Easter. It was one of the first operas to feature historical instead of mythological characters as protagonists and was also among the first operas to be written for a general audience instead of the aristocracy. Whereas Orfeo, Eurydice, and Arianna are sympathetic characters, some of the protagonists of *L'incoronazione di Poppea* are decidedly unsavory: the power-hungry Poppea, above all. In some operas, villains are punished, but in *Poppea*, set in ancient Rome in AD 65, the faithful are humiliated and the morally bankrupt reign triumphant. But for all her distasteful attributes, Poppea is certainly a strong character, and, unlike many operatic heroines to come, she is not dead by curtain call. The real-life Poppea met a worse fate, however: she was kicked to death by the emperor Nero (Nerone) while pregnant.

Act I opens with a poignant aria by Ottone, Poppea's lover, who has returned after an extended absence and discovered that she is having an affair with Nerone. (Nerone has promised to make Poppea queen as soon as he can dispose of his wife, the empress Ottavia.) As in *L'Orfeo*, the way Monteverdi sets the texts to music greatly increases the potency of the words. One of the great moments of baroque opera is the aria "Disprezzata Regina" (Despised queen), in which Ottavia, distressed about her abandonment by Nerone, laments her fate. The different ways Monteverdi sets the words "disprezzata regina" illustrates Ottavia's mood as the aria progresses: at first somber, then anguished, and finally angry. The words "afflitta moglie" (tormented wife) unfold in a descending, sob-like cadence; the phrase "Destin, se stai lassù" (Fate, if you are there), in an anguished outburst. Another example of the brilliant way Monteverdi set text to music is "Addio Roma" (Farewell Rome), which Ottavia—banished from the kingdom—sings before her exile. After a heart-wrenching interlude of strings and organ, she repeats the first syllable of "Addio" with increasing desperation, a cry of anguish echoed by a lone, insistent chord. The opera ends on a sensual note when Poppea is eventually crowned empress. In a ravishing love duet called "Pur ti miro" (I adore you), the voices of Poppea and Nerone intertwine in slow, rapturous bliss.

The word *opera* came into use just before the first performance of *Poppea*, before which operas had been described as "musical tragedy" or "musical drama." Renaissance theater had often included music, but the *Oxford Dictionary of Music* states that music must be integral to an opera in a way that it's not in a play with incidental music. Opera is sung drama, and while there are works (such as Bizet's *Carmen* and Mozart's *Magic Flute*) that include spoken dialogue, you won't hear much straight talking in opera. That means everything is sung, whether "please pass me the margarine" or "I can't live without you, my darling."

Some musicals (like *Les Misérables*) are also sung through. So what's the difference between a musical and an opera? According to the composer Stephen Sondheim, whether a work is classified as an opera or a musical depends in part on how the audience defines it, what listeners expect of it, and even the venue staging it: "The only thing I have to say about the difference between opera and musical theater is that opera is musical theater that takes place in an opera house in front of an opera audience," Sondheim told an interviewer. "This is perhaps not as meaningless as it sounds. The opera audience brings different expectations to what they see and demands different things from the performers, which affects the casting and the approach to the work at hand." Works initially considered musicals, such as Sondheim's *Sweeney Todd*, are now sometimes presented by opera companies. George Gershwin's *Porgy and Bess* (to be discussed in Chapter 5) premiered on Broadway and continues to receive Broadway stagings, but is now usually presented by opera companies; it's often referred to as the "great American opera." The borders are fluid and the debate continues about how, exactly, to classify works of sung drama. There is one crucial difference between musicals and opera, however: in musical theater, the singers are invariably miked, whereas the use of microphones (unless specifically requested by a contemporary composer) is considered rather scandalous in the opera house, although there are occasionally rumors about clandestine use. Opera is all about the sound of the unamplified voice. The music for opera singers also has more highs and lows, literally, than music composed for musical theater. There's a reason people joke about opera singers shattering glass.

There is now little debate about *L'Orfeo*'s status as the first great opera: it succeeded because Monteverdi used music to add depth and poignancy to the story in a way that his contemporaries had failed to do. He also broke new ground in his music by using dissonant harmonies, a forward-looking aesthetic that attracted the ire of his less avant-garde colleagues. Dissonant music usually sounds discordant or jarring, as if the notes don't "belong" together, and is often used to depict turbulent scenes or emotions.

After his death in 1643, *L'Orfeo* and *L'incoronazione di Poppea* gathered dust for centuries until they were resurrected in the late nineteenth century. They are now often performed by period instrument ensembles specializing in music of the Renaissance and baroque that use instruments common in earlier eras. During Monteverdi's lifetime, some integral components of the modern orchestra did not yet exist. Baroque instruments—such as the harpsichord and the viola da gamba (a bowed string instrument)—evolved into instruments with a greater power to project sound. Period instrument ensembles use historical instruments to replicate what would have been heard at the original performances, although, of course, since there are no recordings, it's impossible to know exactly how the music sounded in the baroque period. A specialist ensemble will play baroque music with the musical equivalent of crisp spoken diction, with fleet tempos and a buoyant sound the norm.

Just as orchestral instruments have evolved through the centuries, different voice types are prominent in different eras. Certainly the most unfortunate vocal type in operatic history is the *castrato*, now fortunately extinct. The gruesome practice of castrating boys before puberty to ensure their voices never broke probably stemmed from St. Paul's edict in First Corinthians 14 that women should remain silent in churches. (Females were allowed to sing only in convent choirs.) Along with choirboys, who had a limited shelf life before their voices broke, church ensembles featured *falsettists*. These men sang in falsetto, in which a high sound is produced by using the head voice instead of what is called the chest or full voice. Falsetto has been used by modern singers, too, including Prince, Justin Timberlake, and Radiohead's Thom York. But while most modern singers veer into falsetto for dramatic effect, or to convey tenderness or emotional vulnerability, falsetto singing in the Renaissance had the more practical purpose of creating vocal balance in a choir without women. The roles sung by castrati are now often performed by *mezzo-sopranos* (a female voice type we'll explore later) and *countertenors*, the highest male voice type (who also use falsetto).

Men who sang in falsetto voice were employed in church choirs during the Middle Ages, and by the mid-sixteenth century, castrati had joined their ranks. The falsetto voice was soon deemed inferior to the castrato voice, because, while men singing in falsetto usually can't project or sing very loudly, the castrati demonstrated remarkably powerful voices. They were well trained and rigorously educated in theory, instrumental performance, and singing. Since the education of a castrato wasn't interrupted by puberty, as it was for other male vocalists, they were often ready to make their debuts by their mid- to late teens. The cast of the premiere of Monteverdi's *L'Orfeo* included a castrato who was a musician for the House of Medici. There is little information about the premiere of *L'incoronazione di Poppea*, but it's known that a castrato performed the role of Nerone.

With the flourishing of the new operatic genre, the castrati found a role outside the Catholic Church. Castration was officially illegal, but secular and religious authorities turned a blind eye to the practice, and many poor Italian families subjected their sons to the brutal procedure in the hopes they would escape poverty. If questioned, they might say that their son had suffered an injury—that he'd been attacked by a wild pig or fallen from a horse. The physical appearance of castrati was often unusual because of their lack of testosterone. Only a handful of castrated boys became successful singers, but those who did became the rock stars of the seventeenth and eighteenth centuries. Paid vast sums, they hobnobbed with royalty and were feted by adoring hordes of groupies at their performances. Since they could no longer procreate, the men were forbidden by the Catholic Church from marrying, but they were said to be popular consorts with both men and women, the latter able to enjoy their company without fear of pregnancy.

Some of the castrati were real showbiz divos. A prominent castrato called Marchesi wore a helmet bedecked with extravagant plumes; he liked to make a dramatic stage entrance on horseback, regardless of the opera. The elite castrati, like the legendary singer Farinelli, who died in 1782, demonstrated almost supernatural vocal prowess. They could hold a single note for an extended length, toss off elaborate ornamentation with seemingly little effort, and sing in a remarkably wide and high range. Farinelli was said to enjoy competing with a trumpet player to prove that he could hold a note longer than the brass instrument. But even more than the vocal pyrotechnics, which often elicited thunderous applause, it was the timbre and expressive capabilities of their voices that made listeners swoon. Farinelli, hired to sing at the royal court in Madrid for King Philip V, soothed the melancholy of his royal patron in a private concert every evening. Napoleon officially disapproved of castrati, but he was entranced by their voices nonetheless.

Opera composers stopped writing roles for castrati by the 1830s, and in the late nineteenth century Pope Leo XIII banned the hiring of new castrati for church services. Alessandro Moreschi, the so-called "last castrato," performed until 1913 with the Sistine Chapel Choir. The only recording of a castrato is of Moreschi—but he was past his prime and sounds less than ravishing.

The castrati and their glamorous lives have proven fascinating to many authors and musicians, inspiring innumerable books and stories (by writers including Balzac and Isak Dinesen), along with films, ballets, an opera, and the

Broadway play *Farinelli and the King*. On YouTube, you can watch a scene from the 1994 film *Farinelli*, in which the title character sings a beautiful aria from a Handel opera. The producers of the film used technology to replicate what they imagined a superlative castrato would sound like, blending the voices of a countertenor and a soprano to create a voice of unearthly beauty. In the film, the audience is so moved by Farinelli's voice that listeners shout and swoon. The most gifted castrati seemed to have that effect.

AFTER PERFORMANCES BY THEIR FAVORITE CASTRATI, fans in Italy would sometimes shout "Evviva il coltello!" (Long live the knife!), but in France the singers were ridiculed as cripples. The birth of French opera in the seventeenth century mirrored the origins of Italian opera a few decades earlier. While by the middle of the century, opera in Italy had become a public pastime, with rowdy hordes flocking to public Venetian theaters after the opening of the Teatro San Cassiano, baroque French operas were composed for and designed to flatter Louis XIV. The Italian-born Jean-Baptiste Lully was a favorite of the Sun King and monopolized the Paris and Versailles musical scene between 1672 and 1687 as the director of the Paris Opera, which performed in an ornate theater in the Palais Royal.

Dance was an integral component of French baroque opera, called *tragédie en musique* (tragedy in music) or *tragédie lyrique* (lyric tragedy). The king often participated in the elaborate ballets that were part of the *divertissements* (from the French word for "amusements"), which often featured lavish scenery and costumes. Lully wrote one opera every year, with prologues that referenced important events in Louis XIV's life and plots that unfolded over five acts. Invariably, they were mythological or chivalrous tales of love that alluded to the king's noble character. Despite being officially titled "tragedies," the stories didn't always have sorrowful endings; *tragédie* during the era referred simply to works that treated noble, dignified themes, as opposed to the lighter themes of comedy. The French theatrical tradition had a strong influence on the development of opera in France, and clarity of text was paramount for Lully, who discouraged his singers and instrumentalists from improvising on a particular line, as was common in the Italian opera tradition.

Atys, one of Louis XIV's favorite operas, is currently among the most frequently staged of Lully's thirteen operas, which are now usually presented by specialist companies in productions that sometimes feature sumptuous period costumes and elaborate wigs. The fantastical plots and highly stylized singing and dancing of these operas might strike the spectator as artificial even by operatic standards. But the music, while emotionally restrained compared to the more dramatic extremes of later composers, unfolds with both a stately, regal splendor and a haunting tenderness in moments of tragedy. In *Atys*, which is set to a poetic libretto based on Ovid, the mortal title character is in love with the nymph Sangaride, who is equally enamored of him, but inconveniently betrothed to another.

The jealous goddess Cybèle also has a crush on Atys and puts a spell on him: he is lulled into a deep slumber with a sedative of alluring melodies played by recorders, one of the most beautiful moments in the opera. But there are no sweet dreams for Atys, who is warned by a nightmarish Greek chorus of the dangers of disobeying a goddess. Under the influence of Cybèle's spell, Atys thinks Sangaride is a monster and kills her, ignoring the desperate entreaties of the chorus. Atys attempts suicide when he realizes his terrible mistake, and Cybèle turns him into a tree so she can keep him nearby. Woe betide those who mess with a sorceress in baroque opera! But while sorceresses can (and frequently do) turn men into inanimate objects, they usually fail to control either the human heart or their own emotions.

Power of a different sort appealed to Lully, a bully who monopolized the music scene and prevented talented colleagues from earning their due. He sued one jealous rival on grounds that the man tried to poison him—though in the end, no one needed to stab Lully in the back, because he stabbed himself, puncturing his foot with the baton he was using to conduct a performance honoring the king's good health. After Lully's death in 1687 from the gangrenous infection that ensued, the offstage drama continued between his supporters and those of his successor, Jean-Philippe Rameau, who wrote his first opera in 1733 at age fifty, and for whom Voltaire wrote several librettos. The enemies of Rameau included the philosopher Jean-Jacques Rousseau, an amateur composer whose musical works Rameau scorned as derivative and second-rate.

Just as Monteverdi, with his daring harmonies, had provoked the conservative factions, Rameau—an influential musical theorist and harpsichordist—raised hackles with his own harmonic innovations. He followed the traditional lyric tragedy format but chipped away at Lully's polished veneer with a rawer, less mannered aesthetic that shocked some eighteenth-century listeners. *Hippolyte et Aricie* (*Hippolytus and Aricia*), Rameau's first opera, was based on Jean Racine's play *Phèdre* (*Phaedra*), which in turn had been inspired by the myth of Phaedra, who lusted after her stepson Hippolytus. When Hippolytus rejects her advances, she retaliates by telling her husband, King Theseus of Athens—Hippolytus's father—that he raped her; Theseus then places a curse on Hippolytus, who dies.

Rameau illustrated this tragedy with orchestral music that is denser and richer than Lully's; its virtuoso sections—such as the turbulent flurries of notes that so evocatively depict the storm in Act I—proved challenging for musicians of the era to play. In Act II, when Theseus descends to Hades in an ill-omened mission to rescue a friend, the Furies warn him that Hell awaits him above ground as well. As they sing of their premonitions, Rameau accompanies their warnings with agitated ascending scales. A terrible scene indeed awaits Theseus, who is horrified to find Phaedra and Hippolytus in what appears to be a compromising situation. Theseus misinterprets the situation, thinking his son guilty, even though Hippolytus is disgusted to be the target of his stepmother's passion. Hippolytus is swallowed by a monster in another fiery storm scene; the distraught Phaedra confesses to Theseus that his son was innocent and then poisons herself. Rameau's music so vividly illustrates the traumas of these mythological characters that you feel deeply sorry for them. But the misery evaporates in the final scenes, with recorders and flutes depicting pastoral bliss after Hippolytus is brought back from the dead.

Despite the endless mishaps suffered by the protagonists of baroque opera, everything usually turns out fine in the end. In Henry Purcell's *Dido and Aeneas*, however, the sole masterpiece of English baroque opera, the title heroine does not meet a happy fate. While opera was flourishing on the continent, the genre had a slower start in England, although singing was certainly an integral part of courtly entertainments like the *masque*, which combined music, dance, and poetry. Ironically, the shuttering of theaters during the reign of Oliver Cromwell and the Puritans helped spur the growth of opera in England—a savvy playwright and entrepreneur named William Davenant capitalized on the fact that while the Puritans frowned upon music in church they had not forbidden it in the secular sphere. So he circumvented the ban on theater by setting plays to music, with vocal and instrumental parts written by composers including Matthew Locke. Some of his operas, such as the anti-Catholic *The Cruelty of the Spaniards in Peru*, served as propaganda tools for the Puritans.

Purcell completed *Dido* around 1683, inspired by Virgil's *Aeneid* and the tragic story of Dido, Queen of Carthage. Dido falls in love with the Trojan hero Aeneas when he is shipwrecked en route to build a new Troy, but their burgeoning affair is undone by witches, who trick

Aeneas into abandoning her. Dido expresses her despair in the work's most famous excerpt: "When I am laid in earth," a beautiful lament of stately misery that she sings before killing herself. The aria opens with a mournful bass line that descends with slow gravitas and evokes the image of a coffin being lowered into a grave. "Remember me, remember me, but ah! forget my fate," sings Dido, her imploring cries of "remember me" unfolding in an arc of anguish. It's quite possibly one of the most mournful songs ever written.

THERE ARE ALSO MYRIAD SHADES OF DESPAIR IN THE operas of the composer George Frideric Handel, who was born in Germany, began his career in Italy, and continued to write Italian operas after moving to England. Handel fulfilled the Florentine Camerata's goal of providing listeners with a cathartic experience like that believed to be part of the theatrical experience in ancient Greece, writing music that makes the listener empathize deeply with the characters, however flawed they may be. Handel's works are entrancing because of the technicolor emotional palette his music conveys: rage, despair, passion, and tenderness are evoked with thrilling intensity and sometimes juxtaposed in feverish succession.

Handel composed what is called *opera seria* (serious opera), a dour descriptive that might indicate something staid instead of the lavishly expressive works that are his hallmark. In light of all the vocal pyrotechnics and temperamental outbursts one might wonder what's so "serious" about any of these operas, but the label refers to the subject matter, often tales from ancient history. Opera seria stemmed from efforts by intellectuals who wanted to curb the perceived decadence and immorality of Italian opera. Following in the footsteps of the Florentine Camerata, which had encouraged composers to honor the values of ancient Greek drama, an academy created in 1690 in Rome set out to ensure that opera remained true to its classical roots. The academy urged librettists to write plots featuring characters torn between love, duty, and temptation who eventually choose the moral high ground—unlike the debauched protagonists of Monteverdi's *L'incoronazione di Poppea*, for example.

The poet Pietro Metastasio wrote twenty-seven opera seria librettos that were set hundreds of times by composers working in Italy and elsewhere, including Domenico Scarlatti, Giovanni Battista Pergolesi, Johann Adolph Hasse, Leonardo Vinci, and Nicola Porpora. These operas—which usually had happy endings that flattered the wealthy patrons who commissioned them—are now being revived today by specialist ensembles. Incidentally, while a composer today invariably has more star power than the librettist, in the eighteenth century the librettist received at least equal billing: Metastasio's name was the one in lights.

In addition to disapproving of immoral plots, the Italian reformers also disliked the lavish sets and costumes that the public adored, the onstage mingling of royal and servant characters, the use of common slang, and the popularity of flamboyant star soloists. While many in the twenty-first-century opera world have fretted that opera is too elitist, and spearheaded efforts to attract new audiences, early reformers had the opposite worry: that opera was straying too far from its noble, classical roots, and becoming a popular entertainment. Some of the reformers' lofty aims to sober opera up were realized with the introduction of more elevated language and the exile of comic servant characters. But in other regards, their efforts were stymied by star performers who wanted to show off and not just dutifully reflect on tedious moral quandaries.

While there was an egalitarian element to French baroque opera, with the orchestra, chorus, and multiple soloists all given prominent roles, in eighteenth-century Italian opera divos and divas reigned supreme—too supreme, some thought. The drama took a backseat to these stars, who demanded extravagant arias that would dazzle their listeners. And they didn't want to exit quietly after their turn in the spotlight: they wanted to sing a dramatic *exit aria* that would allow them to leave with a flourish. Handel, working physically and artistically outside the mainstream opera seria tradition in Italy, broadened its artistic parameters substantially with various innovations, although he adhered to the basic formula of the *da capo aria*—an expressive solo song. *Da capo* means "from the beginning" in Italian and is a common term in opera and classical music. A da capo aria has an A-B-A format: the first two sections contrast in mood, and the third is a repeat of the first. The first section (A) is contrasted with the second (and shorter) part (B); the first section (A) is then repeated, with more elaborate ornamentation to keep things interesting. In addition to the da capo arias, opera seria followed a set of fairly strict rules stipulating that the protagonists must have a certain number of arias of contrasting moods. In *rage arias*, the protagonists sing like people in need of anger management therapy, although, since they've often just been abandoned or betrayed, we can usually empathize with their wrath.

There are several rage arias in Handel's opera *Giulio Cesare* (*Julius Caesar*), a loosely historical take on the real-life saga of Cleopatra and Caesar. It proved a hit at its premiere in 1724 and is now frequently staged. In the opera, after the title character arrives in Egypt and vanquishes the armies of his enemy Pompeo, Cornelia (Pompeo's wife) begs Caesar to spare him. He agrees, but Pompeo is killed by the Egyptian king, Tolomeo (Cleopatra's brother). Caesar vents his anger in a rage aria called "Empio dirò, tu sei" (I will say, you are cruel). Caesar calls Tolomeo a villain and fumes against his cruelty after being presented with the severed head of Pompeo as a symbol of surrender. As in Monteverdi, the singing in Handel's operas is sometimes melismatic, with the *á* in the word *crudeltá* (cruelty) heavily ornamented. The melismas are part of an athletic type of singing called *coloratura*, in which a melody is ornamented with trills, runs, and leaps. The best singers use coloratura not to highlight their own virtuosity, but as a way to vividly illustrate the emotional content and text of an aria. Cornelia and her son (Sesto) want revenge: in Sesto's rage aria "Svegliatevi nel core" (Awaken in my heart), he sings of his desire for vengeance and reminisces tenderly about his murdered father. Cleopatra's grief and rage are juxtaposed with manic intensity in her Act III aria "Piangeró la sorte mia" (I shall lament my fate). She dreams of usurping the throne and ruling Egypt: after seducing Caesar, she becomes distraught, because her armies have just lost an important battle and she mistakenly believes that Caesar has died. The word "Piangeró" (I will cry) unfolds with tender introspection. The mood suddenly changes as she dreams of revenge, and then, just as quickly, Cleopatra is again vulnerable and the music plaintive. In contrast to the extravagant rage arias, Handel wrote sparsely ornamented, poignant melodies like that of the duet "Son nato a lagrimar" (I was born to weep)—a moving exchange between Cornelia and Sesto—and the seduction aria "V'adoro, pupille" (I adore you, eyes), in which Cleopatra expresses her vulnerability and love for Caesar in long, sensual lines.

In the opera seria template, da capo arias alternate with *recitativo secco* (dry recitative), dialogue accompanied only by a continuo instrument, such as a harpsichord. These dialogue sections move the action forward, whereas the arias are a chance for the characters to vent, lament, and generally emote. The recitatives can seem dull compared to the arias, although Handel's recitatives are much shorter than those of most other opera seria composers. Conductors who specialize in baroque repertory are adept at aptly pacing the recitative sections so that no musical or dramatic tension is lost.

Cleopatra is one of Handel's most fully developed and nuanced characters, but he rendered many of his other characters—such as the protagonists of *Alcina*, *Ariodante*, and *Orlando*—equally insightfully. The three operas are all based on the Italian epic poem *Orlando furioso* (*The*

Madness of Orlando), about chivalric romance, which was set in the eighth century and published in its entirety in 1532. In *Alcina*—a tale of desperate love woven through with deceptions, illusions, and cross-dressing—the title character is a sorceress who lures knights to her enchanted island and turns them into rocks and trees when she tires of them. One of Alcina's conquests is the knight Ruggiero, who falls for her after she puts a spell on him that makes him immediately forget his fiancée, Bradamante, a feisty knight heroine who dresses in armor to rescue her beloved from various mishaps. In this case, Bradamante dresses as a boy and impersonates her own brother, Ricciardo, in order to rescue Ruggiero, inadvertently winning the amorous attentions of Morgana, Alcina's sister. Ruggiero is so confused about the porous boundaries between truth and fantasy that he is distrustful after learning that "Ricciardo" is actually Bradamante. Ruggiero is given a magic ring that wakes him up to the deceptions, and in the wistful "Verdi prati" (Green meadows) he sings of a beauty he now knows is merely an illusion.

Just like the jealous goddess Cybèle in *Atys*, Alcina finds that her powers are not foolproof when applied either to her own heart or to those she tries to control. She laments her loss of control in "Ah! Mio cor!" (Ah! My heart!), singing of Ruggiero's betrayal. The music is so beautiful and full of anguish that Handel immediately gains our sympathy for Alcina despite her wiles. Whereas we would probably have little sympathy for an online dater whose fake profile led to his or her rejection, Handel makes sure we pity Alcina, who feels wholeheartedly that she is the one deceived. In "Ah! Mio cor!," the eerie vocal and instrumental music evokes the strangeness of this scenario, in which a sorceress—whose job description includes deception and illusion—feels betrayed by a man she bewitched. She may turn her lovers into animals and rocks after she gets bored with them, but only a stony-hearted listener could fail to empathize with her plight. Real love is Alcina's downfall.

Handel's extraordinary music seemed to cast a spell on the first audiences. *Alcina* had a successful run after its premiere in 1735 in a 1,400-seat theater (built on the same site in London where the Royal Opera House is now located). The reigning Handel diva of our era is the American mezzo-soprano Joyce DiDonato, whose virtuosity, like that of any first-rate artist, is always used to heighten the emotional intensity of the music. In a rendition of Alcina's "Ah! Mio cor!" recorded in 2009, the word "Ah" is stretched out in an arc of pain, and the words "Mio cor" unfold with devastating impact. Alcina, who is deeply in love with Ruggiero, has just learned that he is planning to escape. When DiDonato sings "How can you leave me alone and in tears," she conveys the universal pain of heartbreak with such dagger-sharp intensity that Alcina's own foibles seem irrelevant. In a performance of the same aria recorded in 1959 by the Australian soprano Joan Sutherland (who died in 2010), different qualities come to the fore. Whereas DiDonato's fiery, emotive singing highlights Alcina's pain, Sutherland's haunting version illustrates her elusive essence. The different styles of the accompanying orchestras contribute to the mood created by the singers. Il Complesso Barocco, a period-instrument ensemble, performs with the buoyant aesthetic typical of such groups, accompanying DiDonato with a crisply articulated sound that mirrors the emotional heat of her singing. The modern orchestra accompanying Sutherland creates a more languid, mysterious sound that complements her shimmering voice. Both versions are deeply moving.

There's a lot of cross-dressing and gender fluidity in baroque opera and onward. Handel wrote several *trouser roles*, that is, roles for adolescent or young male characters portrayed by women, usually *mezzo-sopranos*. A mezzo sings in the range below a soprano's, which is the closest to a woman's natural speaking voice. Trouser roles, also called pants or breeches roles, include Sesto from *Giulio Cesare*. Baroque opera takes gender fluidity to a level that contemporary audiences interested in the discourse about gender identity might find fascinating. In popular culture today, a low and gruff voice is usually still considered more "masculine" than a high voice, and a male actor with a high-pitched voice is unlikely to be cast as a virile hero in a Hollywood blockbuster. But in the baroque era, castrati would portray conquering heroes and "manly" types like Caesar, roles often now sung by mezzo-sopranos or countertenors. Men also wore clothes that might now be considered "feminine," such as tights, shirts with ruffles, and elaborately decorated waistcoats.

Operas like *Alcina*—a story about the illusions of love—have mind-boggling varieties of gender bending. The role of the dashing knight Ruggiero was written for a castrated man and is now usually sung by a mezzo-soprano, and Bradamante is both a trouser role and a female role.

She's certainly not a typically "feminine" character, in any event, given her penchant for donning armor and dashing off to rescue Ruggiero. Thus in a staged performance we see two women dressed like men declaring their love for each other: one is portraying a man (Ruggiero), and the other is playing a female character who is impersonating her own brother. In typical operatic fashion, the characters fail to recognize their beloveds in "disguise." It's when Bradamante is dressed up like a man that the beautiful Morgana falls for her-him. Confused yet?

The English mezzo-soprano Alice Coote, who specializes in trouser roles, explained the challenges of playing gender-bending roles in an article she wrote for *The Guardian* in 2015. "I have to separate my mind from my body and imagine myself in one with a different gender, structure, sensations, qualities and desires," she wrote. "I have to change my balance and physical movements from the minute to the large. I have to edit my very approach to the world I find myself in and make my interactions and responses male." Coote, who has said that cross-dressing in the theater reveals more about power than gender, has rejected the advice of directors who have suggested she should wear a fake penis under her costumes in order to feel "more male." She has been flattered when audience members have been unaware that a woman was singing, but at the same time, has questioned her own femininity, "and what it consists of, both for me personally and for others, and to ask which part of me defines my female identity, and in what degree. Is it my body, my mind, my chromosomes alone, or the conditioning of society?" Coote has also pointed out that opera, like most other professions, is still largely controlled by men. "Opera is hopefully a democratic process, but sometimes it's a bit too nondemocratic. And this is very much still a male preserve. It's still a man's world. Maybe that's why I like playing men," she told the *New York Times* in 2013.

You rarely have to wait long before someone has a meltdown in opera, which features spectacular *mad scenes* for both male and female characters. Handel pioneered the mad scene in *Orlando*, whose title character becomes deranged by the usual suspect, love. Orlando, a soldier in Charlemagne's army, is smitten with the princess Angelica, but she loves a prince, and Orlando goes insane with jealousy. The magician Zoroastro encourages him to focus on the battlefield instead, but Orlando doesn't want to choose between love and duty. He rants, raves, and mourns in a hallucinatory trip to the underworld. By the end of the scene, Orlando lets loose with a tirade in which his impassioned outbursts are propelled by the orchestra's angry flourishes. The music echoes the various shades of Orlando's derangement with remarkable nuance.

There are fewer mad scenes, but certainly plenty of passionate singing, in Handel's *oratorios*, which he wrote for the burgeoning middle class after enthusiasm began to wane for the Italian librettos and complicated plots of opera seria. One main difference between an oratorio and an opera is that the former is conceived for concert presentations (usually without costumes, props, or movement) and the latter for a staged production. Handel's oratorios, including his famous *Messiah*, feature English librettos and are usually based on stories from the Old Testament that would have been familiar to his audience. *Messiah*, known for its rousing "Hallelujah" chorus and now a popular Christmas staple, was first performed during Easter and attracted such huge audiences that ladies were requested not to wear hoop skirts to avoid overcrowding. Handel also wrote English-language works based on mythology, such as *Semele*—a tale of adulterous love that shocked audiences during its Lent premiere. While oratorios were intended for the concert hall, some of these theatrical pieces, including *Semele*, are now presented as fully costumed and staged works by opera houses. Most of Handel's operas and oratorios fell into near obscurity after his death but were revived in the mid-twentieth century. The revival shows no sign of abating, fortunately, and there are now bountiful opportunities to hear his operas performed live.

WHILE DA CAPO ARIAS LIKE ALCINA'S "AH! MIO COR!" ARE splendid in their depiction of emotions like love and rage, the more flamboyant elements of such arias, and the opera seria tradition in general, irked the German composer Christoph Willibald Gluck, yet another reformer on a mission to make opera behave properly. He scorned what he saw as abuses of the art form committed by baroque composers. In the preface to his opera *Alceste*, he derided "the ignorant vanity of singers" and "the excessive complaisance of composers," both of which he thought had "disfigured Italian Opera and turned the most splendid and most beautiful of spectacles into the most ridiculous and tiresome." For Gluck, the showy da capo arias were little more than unseemly vocal bling; he strove instead for music that would express "the true meaning of the poetry" in a beautiful and simple manner. He and his fellow reformers reined in peacock singers by creating few opportunities for them to flaunt their vocal feathers, and further diminished their star-power by composing music that flowed continuously, with scant pause for applause. But whereas earlier reformers wanted to curtail the growth of opera as a popular entertainment, and return it to its aristocratic and exclusive roots, Gluck followed Handel's example, composing with the expanding middle class in mind, a move that reflected the broader cultural and political shifts of the time.

During Gluck's lifetime, there were heated tussles, both verbal and physical, between his supporters and the champions of Niccolò Piccinni, an Italian composer who was invited to Paris by Gluck's detractors. (Neither composer encouraged the rival gangs.) Benjamin Franklin, who was visiting Paris at the height of these musical turf wars, wrote in a letter to a friend: "Happy people! You live certainly under a wise, just and mild government, since you have no public grievances to complain of, nor any subject of contention but the perfections and imperfections of foreign music." Gluck wrote a number of works in typical opera seria format, then broke new ground with *Orfeo ed Euridice* (*Orpheus and Eurydice*), his first collaboration with the poet and librettist Ranieri Calzabigi. Gluck may have sounded like a Puritan spoilsport in his quest to "reform" Italian opera, but his efforts resulted in a truly beautiful opera.

Like dressmakers altering an outfit for a new customer, composers often tailored their works for different audiences and singers: Gluck wrote two versions of *Orfeo*, one for Vienna and a later version for Paris; the latter featured a tenor instead of a castrato and more of the dance interludes that pleased French audiences. Gluck's "reform" operas do not have da capo arias, and the recitative sections are accompanied by a full orchestra. This *recitativo accompagnato* (accompanied recitative) replaced the bare-bones continuo accompaniment of recitativo secco (dry recitative) that was then typical of Italian opera—and often so tedious that listeners would entertain themselves until the da capo showpieces. The chorus, which had a negligible role in opera seria, is an important component of Gluck's *Orfeo*, which begins after Euridice has already been bitten by the snake. A choir of nymphs and shepherds laments her death, and their grief is punctuated by Orfeo's heartbroken cries of his beloved's name. The chorus, embodying the Furies in Act II, expresses anger at Orfeo's brazen descent to their world: the strings play rapidly ascending and descending minor scales as the Furies sing of letting Orfeo hear the "hounds of hell howl in the night." He urges them to "turn away your rage," but his plea and the sweet timbre of his lyre—a gentle contrast to their ire—is interrupted by their dissonant outbursts. When Orfeo leads Euridice out of Hades and loses her again after illicitly turning back to look at her, he sings an aria called "Che faro senza Euridice?" (What shall I do without Eurydice?). The "beautiful simplicity" that Gluck strove for is achieved in the eloquent, melancholic words and in the melody of this poignant song. Everything turns out fine in the end: Orfeo is reunited with Euridice, and the chorus, representing the nymphs and shepherds, sings of the triumph of love.

Gluck had a significant influence on his successors, including Mozart, who brought love back to earth with human characters whose trials on the path to love are every bit as fraught as Orfeo's. Baroque composers depicted universal emotions such as rage and despair in a way that allows us to share the joys and sorrows of a sorceress or a Hades-bound musician, even if we can't really relate to such characters. Since the focus was mostly on abstract emotions, composers and singers would sometimes use arias like musical hand-me-downs that allowed generic characters to convey one-size-fits-all emotions, or gave a star singer a chance to recycle a favorite aria from one opera into another. But Mozart tailored his music to psychologically complex characters and created relatable scenarios—such as an engaged couple questioning their commitment, or a lecherous married boss lusting after an employee. His operas depict human protagonists with a depth unseen in baroque opera.

When the lecherous Count in *The Marriage of Figaro* apologizes to his wife, Mozart accompanies this plea for forgiveness with music of such sincerity that it's easy to understand why the Countess forgives him: the music makes us believe that the apology must be genuine. In *Don Giovanni*, the noblewoman Donna Elvira knows the title character is a treacherous jerk, but she pines for him anyway, torn between wanting revenge and worrying about his fate. She could be depicted as a character worthy of scorn, merely a battered woman with low self-esteem who can't let go. People don't instantly fall out of love just because someone has wronged them, however, and Mozart's music elicits our sympathy for this very human situation. And it's the music that illustrates the painful truths behind the seemingly farcical story of *Così fan tutte* (*All Women Are Like That*, or *Thus Do They All*): people are complicated, unknowable, and full of surprises.

In his first decade of life, Mozart, born in Salzburg, Austria, in 1756, wrote symphonies and sonatas. At age eleven he composed his first opera, the remarkably accomplished *Apollo et Hyacinthus* (*Apollo and Hyacinth*). His father, Leopold Mozart, a court violinist and mediocre composer in Salzburg, was a tireless stage dad who taught his son to play various instruments. (Leopold and his wife, Anna Maria, lost five of their seven children in infancy.) He took the young Wolfgang and his sister Nannerl on extensive tours of Europe to show them off to heads of state and royalty, exposing his son to a range of music. When the junior Mozart died at thirty-five, he left a huge catalog of works. In addition to twenty-two operas, it includes some forty symphonies, sonatas for solo keyboard, and innumerable works for chamber ensembles. Mozart died before completing his final work, the majestic and very operatic Requiem in D minor. When used to describe a person, the word "operatic" could be negative, implying a histrionic or melodramatic person, but in the context of music it's a compliment. If someone describes a symphony or piano sonata as "operatic," it's probably a work full of drama and contrast and music that moves the heartstrings. There is an "operatic" quality to much of Mozart's nonvocal music, in the songful melodic lines, the dramatic contours, and the vivid dialogue between different instruments. In the Sonata for Piano and Violin in E minor, for example, the dialogue unfolds between the two instruments with tempestuous fervor until the final movement, when the key briefly changes from minor to major. The piano plays a simple repeated chord, beginning a melody that is taken up by the violin and evokes a tender reunion after the stormy outbursts. It's easy to imagine these melodic lines sung by two lovers in one of Mozart's operas.

There is no joyful embrace awaiting the spurned Princess Elettra at the end of Mozart's *Idomeneo* (*Idomeneus*), however, an opera seria he wrote at age twenty-four, and which marked a turning point in his career. Although the mythological story line was traditional, he broke new ground with daring harmonies, inventive orchestral music, and complex psychological portraits that differed from the traditional allegorical and universal characters and emotions of opera seria. In the opera, Elettra loves Idamante (the son of Idomeneo, King of Crete), but he is smitten with the captured Trojan princess Illia. Idamante and Illia live happily ever after, while poor Elettra is left in despair. She expresses her misery in a powerful recitative called "Oh smania! oh furie!" (Oh frenzy! oh Furies!), which begins with her tortured, self-pitying visions of Idamante in the arms of her rival. In the aria "D'Oreste, d'Ajace" (Orestes and Ajax), she fumes and invokes fearsome reptiles, expressing a very human array of conflicting emotions. The orchestra mirrors her distress with music that sounds by turns anxious and outraged.

Mozart disagreed with Monteverdi about the relative importance of text and music: whereas Monteverdi had deemed text the mistress of harmony, Mozart wrote, in a letter to his father in 1781, that "in an opera the poetry must absolutely be the obedient daughter of the music." Why, he asked, "are Italian comic operas so successful everywhere—in spite of those wretched librettos?...Because in them the music reigns supreme, and you forget everything else." Mozart had rejected the first draft of the text for *Idomeneo* as too cumbersome, but his music met its match in the brilliant librettos of Lorenzo Da Ponte, with whom he collaborated on three works now known as the Mozart–Da Ponte trilogy: *The Marriage of Figaro*, *Don Giovanni*, and *Così fan tutte*. The pair elevated the genre of *opera buffa*—eighteenth-century Italian comic opera featuring stock characters that represent ordinary folk in commonplace situations—into masterpieces blending comedic and tragic elements with an almost unrivaled sophistication.

Da Ponte, born in 1749 near Venice to a Jewish family, converted to Catholicism when he was fourteen. He studied several languages, including Greek, Latin, and Hebrew, at a local seminary, and committed to the priesthood in order to fund his seminary studies. He was ordained at twenty-four, although he described the priesthood as "wholly contrary to my temperament, my character, my principles, and my studies." Indeed, his womanizing and generally debauched lifestyle, along with several seditious poems he wrote that irked the authorities, led to him being charged with "public concubinage," among other things, and exiled from Venice. His friends included Casanova.

Eventually Da Ponte immigrated to America to escape his myriad affairs, unpaid debts, and irate foes—one of whom, ostensibly trying to assist him with dental problems, had given him nitric acid to dab on his gums. In New York he worked as a grocer and taught Italian at Columbia College. He was a champion of Italian opera in the New World until his death at eighty-nine.

As a librettist working in Europe, Da Ponte produced texts for several composers, including Antonio Salieri, who was depicted in *Amadeus*, the film adapted by Milos Forman and Peter Shaffer from the latter's play. During one scene we see Salieri seething with jealousy as Mozart sits at the keyboard and transforms a boring march Salieri had written in his honor into something much more imaginative, having heard it only once. While the film certainly took artistic liberties, Mozart was indeed able to play back music after a single hearing, a talent he had demonstrated as a small child, when he would listen to his sister Nannerl practicing and then play the same music himself, even before he knew how to read a score. In the fictional cinematic scene, Mozart plays Salieri's boring tune and turns it into the livelier melody heard in the aria "Non più andrai, farfallone amoroso" (You won't go anymore, amorous butterfly), from *Le nozze di Figaro* (*The Marriage of Figaro*).

Mozart and Da Ponte based this opera (their first collaboration) on a subversive play that mocked the aristocracy, something unthinkable for their predecessors, who had little choice but to flatter their patrons. Pierre Beaumarchais's play *La folle journée, ou Le mariage de Figaro* (*The Mad Day, or The Marriage of Figaro*), had initially been banned from public performance by Louis XVI because it irreverently depicted the aristocracy as corrupt, but the play was widely praised when it finally premiered in Paris in 1784. It had also been banned in Vienna, where, in addition to having concerns about its political overtones, the authorities disliked what they saw as its sexual innuendos and moral failings (it depicted, for example, an affair between a lowly page and the Countess). Da Ponte, who had landed a plum job as the librettist for the court theater of Emperor Joseph II a few years after being exiled from Venice, managed to convince the censors that he would maintain propriety in his libretto, and was granted rights to turn the play into an opera, which premiered to acclaim in 1786 in Vienna. In deference to his employer, Da Ponte had toned down some politically provocative elements of the Beaumarchais play and omitted Figaro's tirade against the Count, in which the servant rails against the unearned privileges of the nobility and touts the cunning and intelligence needed by the common man. In the opera, Figaro instead sings a diatribe against women, lambasting them as "thorny roses," "cunning vixens," and "masters of deceit."

The Marriage of Figaro explores the tensions between the "one percent" and the masses, a topic as relevant for our time as it was before the French Revolution. Love and lust in various guises (and disguises) are also themes of the opera, which unfolds over a single tumultuous day in which the nuptials of the servants Figaro and Susanna are nearly thwarted by the Count and other complications. The Count lusts after Susanna, and even though he has ostensibly renounced his feudal *droit du seigneur*, an ancient tradition in which the master of the estate claimed the right to bed women in his service, she suspects that he may try and sleep with her nonetheless. There are quick-witted, comic scenes as the servants try to thwart the Count, and the Countess is wooed by the perpetually horny teenage page Cherubino as she tries to win back her husband (who is jealous despite his own philandering). Thrown into the plot are several stock characters, including the music teacher Don Basilio, the lawyer Dr. Bartolo, and his housekeeper, Marcellina (who turns out to be Figaro's long-lost mother).

In Act I, Mozart sets the tone for the upcoming battle of wits between the classes with "Se vuol ballare" (If you want to dance). The opening lyrics of this *cavatina* (a short aria of one or two sections) are set to a seemingly innocuous minuet, the stately dance of aristocrats. Figaro, aware that the Count is hitting on Susanna, declares in a sardonic manner that he will outwit his lecherous master: he will call the tune and not the other way round. In "Non più andrai" (the tune heard in the film *Amadeus*), Figaro teases Cherubino, saying the young man's flirtatious existence will soon end in the army: the string instruments evoke a flitting butterfly, and a lighthearted fanfare evokes military life. The many comedic moments in the opera are interwoven with a genuine melancholy about human relationships, as when the despairing Countess mourns her broken marriage in the aria "Porgi, amor, qualche ristoro" (Grant, love, some comfort). She sings, "Love, give me back my treasure, / or at least let me die," with the rich, dark-hued sounds of clarinets providing a sensual accompaniment to her introverted lament. In her aria "Dove sono i bei momenti?" (Where are the beautiful moments?), the Countess reminisces sadly about the sweet times she and the philandering Count shared together. But despite his wrongdoings, she still loves him, and she hopes to win him back with a ploy involving Susanna (her maid).

In addition to such beautiful arias, Mozart wrote remarkable music in his operas for vocal ensembles. When a group of people talk at once, the result is invariably cacophonous, as we see all too often when talking heads compete for attention on cable news shows. But in opera, when multiple characters sing differing opinions and feelings together it magnifies the emotional nuances of a particular scene in a sonically gorgeous way. There are heart-wrenching duos in early opera, like "Pur ti miro" (I adore you) in Monteverdi's *L'incoronazione di Poppea*, but on the whole there was little scope for larger ensembles in the da-capo aria and recitative format of opera seria. Mozart composed music for larger groups of protagonists, writing different music for individuals to sing simultaneously in a way that functions as a richly layered theatrical device.

The twenty-minute Act II finale of *The Marriage of Figaro* starts with a duet between the Count and Countess and builds to a septet as various characters appear. The Count thinks Cherubino and the Countess are having an affair and tries to enter the closet where he thinks the young man is hiding, but Cherubino has escaped out the window and Susanna has taken his place. The voices of the surprised Count and Countess join with Susanna's in a trio of confusion. Figaro's voice is added to the fray when he shows up and demands to marry Susanna; soon after, in a prayerful-sounding trio, Figaro, the Countess, and Susanna implore the Count to let the marriage proceed. Things get even more chaotic when the gardener, Antonio, makes an appearance, upset that Cherubino has smashed his flowerpot while leaping from the balcony. Figaro, Susanna, and the Countess form a united front against Antonio and the suspicious Count. The chaos increases yet further when the vengeful Marcellina, supported by Basilio and Bartolo, demands that Figaro marry her instead of Susanna as payment for a debt. "Softly now, without this clamor, / let everyone speak his mind," urges the Count, declaring that he will be the one to render judgment. Everyone simultaneously sings his or her mind, so to speak, the seven voices overlapping in a gorgeous blend as they all state their case. Another ensemble scene concludes the four-act opera after the Countess forgives the Count. Their heartfelt moment is echoed by the ensemble of protagonists, who observe that "only love can resolve / this day of torments," their somber proclamation quickly dissolving into a joyous call to celebration. The old romantic and hierarchical orders are at least temporarily restored. Even if love and fidelity will soon again be fleeting, as Mozart seems to hint, forgiveness is essential.

Certainly, the character of Don Giovanni—the womanizer of the second work in the Mozart–Da Ponte trilogy—seems particularly timeless on the heels of the #MeToo movement in our day. Like the long list of wealthy and powerful men fired in 2017 for harassing women, Don Giovanni meets his downfall. The legend of Don Giovanni had already inspired many plays and musical works: in 1787, the year Mozart wrote his opera (subtitled *Il dissoluto punito*, or *The Dissolute Punished*), three Don Giovanni operas were produced in Italy. Nineteenth-century critics lavished praise on Mozart's version, which the writer Gustave Flaubert deemed one of the three finest things God ever made (the other two being the sea and *Hamlet*). But despite the fact that Don Giovanni is an amoral man— who assaults women and murders men—musically, Mozart saves his judgment for the end, depicting Giovanni as an ambiguous, even charming character, and giving him no introspective arias to reflect on his actions or their consequences. In the exuberant "Champagne Aria," Giovanni seems more irresistible rogue than liar and assassin: in tongue-twisting speed he orders his servant, Leporello, to plan a feast, gather girls, and get everyone drunk— boasting, in tuneful, locker-room banter, that he'll have another ten notches on the bedpost by morning.

We're aware from the opening moments of the opera that this will not end well, however. Thunderous, apocalyptic chords and ominous ascending and descending scales in the overture hint at the turbulence of upcoming scenes. (In opera, the *overture* is a short introduction that sets the tone of the story and sometimes introduces musical themes.) Then the music suddenly sounds more upbeat, juxtaposing the moods that define the opera. The story, set in Seville, begins on a sinister note when Giovanni tries to escape from the home of Donna Anna, a noblewoman he has just sexually assaulted. She calls him a villain, and her screams awaken her father, the Commendatore, whom the remorseless Giovanni kills in a duel. (A *commendatore* is a member of an Italian honorary military order.) Mozart's music reflects the character and desires of each protagonist. Don Ottavio is Donna Anna's loyal, kind fiancé: the archetypal good guy whose primary concern is the happiness of his sweetheart. Mozart gives him sweet-natured music, and his declarations of love unfold in long, languid phrases. In the duo "Fuggi, crudele, fuggi!" (Flee, cruel one, flee!), Donna Anna and Ottavio swear they will avenge the Commendatore's death. Anna is distraught, and the music reflects her fiery personality and quest for vengeance, a contrast to the good-natured and lilting music accompanying Ottavio, who can scarcely believe a nobleman like Giovanni capable of such crimes.

Like the Countess, Donna Anna retains her dignity in grief, as when she demands that Ottavio avenge her honor, singing "Or sai chi l'onore / Rapire a me volse" (Now you know who wanted / to rob me of my honor). On the other hand, the vengeful Donna Elvira, who fell in love with Giovanni before being abandoned by him, is driven mad by his betrayal. In the accompanied recitative and coloratura aria "In quali eccessi...Mi tradi quell'alma ingrata" (In what excesses...This ungrateful scoundrel betrayed me), Mozart vividly evokes the confusion of the love-struck Donna Elvira, who feels a demonic fury at his betrayal and yet worries about his fate. Leporello provides most of the comic relief and (like Figaro) rants against the burdens of his job, which include acting as watchman out in the cold during his master's amorous encounters. In the "Catalogue Aria," Leporello tallies up his master's bedpost notches:

Giovanni, he tells Elvira, has bedded 640 women in Italy, 231 in Germany, and 1003 in Spain, among them

country wenches,
chambermaids and city ladies,
countesses, baronesses,
marchionesses, princesses,
[and] women of every social class,
every shape, and every age.

One of Giovanni's targets is Zerlina (a peasant girl engaged to Masetto), who is momentarily dazzled by Giovanni's class, wealth, and compliments.

Just as in *The Marriage of Figaro*, in *Don Giovanni* Mozart wrote brilliant ensemble scenes, deftly mixing comedy and tragedy in a tumultuous sextet in Act II. Donna Elvira pines for Giovanni, Donna Anna mourns her murdered father, Don Ottavio tries to comfort her, and Leporello (who has been impersonating Giovanni) tries to escape the scene only to be decried as the murderer by the other characters. Elvira begs them to spare his life, forcing Leporello to reveal his true identity, resulting in everyone's confusion. Giovanni eventually pays for his sins: after being reprimanded by the ghost of the Commendatore and refusing to repent, he is dragged down to Hell. The opera concludes with an uplifting ensemble number in which everyone sings about the fate of evildoers. The music is emphatically victorious in temperament: while Mozart does not use music to condemn Giovanni during the opera, in the final moments judgment is unequivocal. This is the end all sinners meet, they sing: malicious sinners will eventually be punished.

Don Giovanni is a role for a baritone, a man who sings in the range below the tenor voice. The word "baritone" is derived from the Greek word *barýtonos*, which means "deep sounding." When describing a singer's voice, opera commentators often use adjectives also used by wine connoisseurs, such as creamy, sparkling, elegant, earthy, big, lean, dusky, velvety, sweet, supple, rich, and so forth. These descriptive terms are on one level subjective, because what sounds pleasantly "bright" to one listener might seem "shrill" to another. There's also the intangible element of vocal charisma: you need to be able to hear Don Giovanni's swagger and charm in his voice, for example. The Swedish baritone Peter Mattei has an elegant, burnished voice that is remarkably beautiful, but that's not enough to create a convincing portrayal of a charming Casanova. Mattei (who also happens to be tall and charismatic on stage) sings the fast-paced Champagne Aria with an ease and charm that convey the indefatigable energy of his libidinous character. Mattei's voice also sounds sensual: he's an irresistible smooth-talker in the duet "La ci darem la mano" (There we will take each other's hands), in which Giovanni attempts to seduce Zerlina.

For Don Giovanni, all women are the same in one sense: whatever their age, nationality, or appearance, he sees them merely as targets. In the other two Da Ponte operas, women are the libidinous, supposedly unfaithful ones: in *The Marriage of Figaro*, Don Basilio declares that all pretty women are fickle. The jealous Count rails against women's untrustworthiness when he (wrongly) suspects his wife, and after declaring that it's always madness to trust a woman, Figaro lets loose in a misogynist tirade. The two young male protagonists of *Così fan tutte* are goaded into testing their fiancées' fidelity. The opera was originally given the full title of *Così fan tutte, ossia La Scuola degli Amanti* (*All Women Are Like That, or The School for Lovers*), but is now shortened to *Così fan tutte*. If a dark thread of deception is woven through *The Marriage of Figaro*, an even more ominous undercurrent propels *Così*, the final collaboration between Mozart and Da Ponte. Although *Don Giovanni* was widely praised by intellectuals, the artificiality of the *Così* libretto—with its farcical scenes of mistaken identities—was much derided in the nineteenth century by luminaries including Beethoven, Wagner, and Goethe. Mozart was criticized for giving a seemingly trite story music of gravitas and beauty, and yet it is the music that reveals the depth of what may initially seem frivolous in this opera, becoming the engine of a story that for all its slapstick moments and comic intrigue ultimately offers a stark glimpse into human nature and relationships.

Ferrando and Guglielmo (two young officers in Naples) extol the virtue of their fiancées (the sisters Fiordiligi and Dorabella). The cynical Don Alfonso warns the men that all women are unfaithful and convinces them to test the girls' fidelity. At his urging, the two men pretend they've been called up to the army, and the couples bid each other farewell with romantic zeal. Interwoven with their heartfelt "addios" are snarky asides from Alfonso, who sings to himself that he can barely restrain himself from bursting out into laughter. The sisters, unaware that it's all a setup, are joined by Alfonso and bid the men a smooth voyage in "Soave sia il vento" (May the wind be gentle). Mozart takes the sisters' distress at the departure seriously: unlike in the Farewell Quintet, there is nothing sarcastic in this lovely, innocent, and entirely uncynical-sounding trio. The fiancés return disguised as "Albanians" and hit on each other's girlfriends, who are encouraged by their maid (Despina) to flirt with the new suitors. But Fiordiligi is troubled by her feelings, and again, Mozart takes the situation seriously. In the tender "Per pietà, ben mio, perdona" (Please, my beloved, forgive), she sings of her determination to crush her illicit desire. She declares that Guglielmo, her fiancé, deserves better than her, unaware that he's off cavorting with Dorabella. But eventually the two sisters decide to marry the "foreigners"—and of course are startled to learn soon afterward that they are actually Ferrando and Guglielmo.

After much confusion and chaos, all ends well. As in *The Marriage of Figaro*, everyone is reunited with his or her original, and appropriate, partner. The two couples join Despina and Alfonso in an upbeat sextet in which they agree to follow Alfonso's advice: forgive, laugh, find equilibrium, and make reason their guide. But while this jovial finale might seem rather artificial, there's nothing superficial about the underlying conclusions. Amid all the larks and comedy, the naïveté of these young lovers has been shattered. They have each discovered truths about themselves—and had a chance to witness their partner in a very different light.

In his final opera, *Die Zauberflöte* (*The Magic Flute*), Mozart also explores the journey toward physical and spiritual love. This opera is a *singspiel*, a form of German-language opera popular in the late eighteenth century that features musical numbers linked by extended sections of spoken dialogue and stage activity. Mozart had written one successful singspiel earlier in his career, the comic *Die Entführung aus dem Serail* (*The Abduction from the Seraglio*), about a Spanish woman and her English maid captured by a Turkish pasha for his harem. The opera reflected the Viennese trend for Turkish music. *The Magic Flute* is a fairy-tale allusion to Freemasonry, an important social movement in the Enlightenment that emphasized integrity, human rights, and education, but was disliked by wary authoritarian European monarchs and the church. Mozart was a member; other famous Freemasons included Benjamin Franklin and Voltaire. The opera (which has a libretto by Emanuel Schikaneder) is about the battle between good and evil and different kinds of love, and like Mozart's other operas, it is both comic and profound.

The Magic Flute is set in an ancient pseudo-Egypt and prominently features the number three (significant in Freemasonry): the overture opens with three dramatic chords, the story includes a trio of child spirits, and Prince Tamino must overcome three trials imposed by the priest Sarastro—one of which includes a vow of silence. Tamino's paramour, Pamina, is hurt by his seeming indifference, just like Eurydice is wounded by Orfeo's silence. There are also Three Ladies, who serve the evil Queen of the Night, Pamina's mother. Whereas in the Da Ponte operas, relationships between the sexes are fraught and all too human, love in *The Magic Flute* is idealized. The bird-catcher Papageno (a comic character) and Pamina both dream of marriage and declare that they live for love in the gentle, innocent-sounding duo "Bei Männern, welche Liebe fühlen" (In men, who feel love). Papageno finds love with Papagena, his ideal match. Aided by the magic flute, Tamino and Pamina eventually overcome their trials, are united, and attain enlightenment.

The Commendatore in *Don Giovanni* and Sarastro in *The Magic Flute* are roles for *bass* voices—the lowest male voice type. In Sarastro's solemn aria "O Isis und Osiris" (O Isis and Osiris), in which he asks the gods to bless Tamino and Pamina as they begin their journey to enlightenment, the vocal line descends with mystical gravitas into its lowest register. Both male and female speaking voices deepen with age, and we associate low voices with authority and experience. (The British prime minister Margaret Thatcher studied with a speech coach to lower the pitch of her voice in order to sound more commanding.) In opera, basses often sing authoritative roles such as priests, fathers, and kings. The Queen of the Night's famous aria "Der Hölle Rache" (Hell's vengeance) is the other end of the vocal spectrum from Sarastro's: as she urges Pamina to kill Sarastro, her voice catapults toward a high F in one of the most stratospheric, deranged-sounding passages in opera.

Some male singers with low voices are classified as *bass-baritones*, a type of voice that has a broader range, spanning both bass and baritone, and the timbral qualities of each. There is some flexibility with roles for low voices in Mozart operas: Don Giovanni, for example, can be sung by a baritone, a bass-baritone, or a bass. Within each vocal range—bass, baritone, tenor, and countertenor for men, and contralto, mezzo-soprano, and soprano for women—there are multiple subcategories. The range of the voice, along with its weight, color, and timbre, helps determine which roles a singer is best suited to perform, a method of categorization known as the *Fach* system. Just as body type will render an athlete better suited to a particular sport or position on a team, voice types are associated with certain composers, genres, and roles, and most singers specialize accordingly. In general, a singer who performs heavyweight Romantic and early twentieth-century roles is probably going to be as uncomfortable on Handel's coloratura treadmill as a linebacker would be doing pirouettes on the beam, although a handful of singers have spanned diverse roles.

A *soubrette* is the lightest soprano voice and has a sweet timbre well suited for flirtatious young girls in comic operas as well as servant or peasant characters, such as Zerlina in *Don Giovanni*. Soubrettes often graduate to different roles as their voices develop, though a sassy young character like Zerlina clearly requires a different vocal quality than a wronged woman like Donna Anna. A *lyric tenor* has a light voice suitable for the mild-mannered tenor roles in Mozart's operas, such as Don Ottavio. Lyric sopranos usually have a clear, bright timbre and are sympathetic characters, like Susanna in *The Marriage of Figaro*. A coloratura mezzo-soprano, soprano, or tenor has the agility to navigate the florid music of baroque and early nineteenth-century Italian opera. The operatic voice changes with age just as the spoken voice does and occasionally a singer will change vocal category entirely: Plácido Domingo switched to baritone repertory after a long and distinguished career as a tenor. While older operatic characters, such as priests and kings, are rarely portrayed by the youngest singers, artists well into middle age and beyond sometimes perform the roles of teenage girls and virile lovers—one of many situations in opera demanding the suspension of disbelief.

George Bernard Shaw once described opera as "when a tenor and soprano want to make love, but are prevented from doing so by a baritone." While the tenor was usually relegated to the boring good guy roles in Mozart's operas, with the baritone the star of the show, in early nineteenth-century Italian opera the tenor took center stage as the virile romantic lead. For Bellini, Rossini, and Donizetti and their colleagues, there was no debate about the relative merits of music or poetry. The voice reigned supreme.

CHAPTER 2

THE BEAUTIFUL SONG OF ITALIAN OPERA

ON THE BEL CANTO OPERAS OF BELLINI, ROSSINI, AND DONIZETTI AND THE RISE OF THE TENOR

BEL CANTO TRANSLATES AS "BEAUTIFUL SINGING" OR "beautiful song." You might logically assume that all opera is about beautiful singing, but the term usually refers to both a particular style of singing and a genre of early nineteenth-century Italian opera. In bel canto operas, the voice is paramount. "Opera, through singing," wrote the Sicilian composer Vincenzo Bellini in 1834, "must make one weep, shudder, die." A key element of bel canto singing is *legato*—which means that notes must be smoothly connected and the singer must shift seamlessly between different registers of the voice. Legato is the opposite of *staccato*—extremely short and detached notes, like those of "Chopsticks." The bel canto genre features long, flowing melodic lines and (as in baroque music) highly florid, ornamented passages. Picture how the ribbons in a rhythmic gymnastics routine unfurl in ornately decorative but seamless lines, and imagine the vocal equivalent. Legato is also an important element in piano music of the era: pianists who play nocturnes by Frédéric Chopin (a friend of Bellini's) aim to create a "singing" tone and ensure that the long melodies unfurl smoothly.

While some bel canto composers churned out dozens of operas, Bellini—who died in 1835 at thirty-three—wrote only ten. He is best known for *Norma*, which premiered in 1831 and remains a bel canto benchmark. Norma is a psychologically complex character who faces the common operatic conundrum of being torn between duty and passion. Hers are also very female dilemmas: she must navigate societal, religious, friendship, and parental obligations that seem impossible to reconcile with her amorous desires. Bellini's librettist (Felice Romani) was inspired by *Norma, ou L'infanticide* (*Norma, or The Infanticide*), a tragic play by the French poet and dramatist Alexandre Soumet. The story mostly takes place in a temple and a forest in Gaul (present-day France) shortly after the occupation by the Romans. The Druids hope that Norma (their high priestess) will encourage a revolt against the despised Roman occupiers, but she advises against rebellion. Her followers are unaware that she is committing treason and has broken her vow of chastity by having an affair with the Roman proconsul Pollione, with whom she has two children.

In Act I, Norma sings "Casta Diva" (Chaste Goddess), perhaps the most famous bel canto aria and certainly one of the most poignant. The beautiful melody in this prayer to the moon goddess and plea for peace is first played by wind instruments, then taken up by the voice. The words "casta diva" unfold with hymn-like solemnity in a long, unbroken phrase that floats above the ensemble. The violins support the vocal line with a slowly arpeggiated chord played in unison, then the lower strings add a gentle *pizzicato* (a note that is plucked instead of bowed) at the beginning of each chord. The orchestral music in this particular aria is simple and transparent, a suitably mystical accompaniment to a prayer so ethereal it would seem hard for any deity to resist.

But with its incongruous pairing of somber lyrics and upbeat accompaniment, the oom-pah-pah structure of bel canto orchestral music can also sometimes sound simplistic. In the confrontation scene at the end of Act I, for example, a young priestess, Adalgisa, and Norma discover, to their horror, that they are both in love with Pollione. In the trio "Oh! di qual sei tu vittima" (Oh! You are the victim), as Norma tells Adalgisa that she has been the victim of such a horrific deception that she'd be better off dead, their distressed outbursts are accompanied by a cheery waltz that imbues this devastating scene with an odd bounciness. And when Norma accuses Pollione of being a traitor, the words are so caustic and the music so cheery that it seems as if the composer and the librettist got a few wires crossed. But in the beginning of Act II, the orchestra and the singer sound once again like they're on the same page. A wistful cello melody reflects Norma's sadness as she contemplates murdering her offspring, because she'd rather they be dead than have to live in shame without a father. In a tender recitative, her desperate words framed by melancholy orchestral sighs, she observes that they are both sleeping and won't see her lift her hand against them.

Infanticide is a grisly recurring theme in opera, but fortunately Norma decides not to murder her children. She also can't bring herself to kill Pollione when given the chance. In the end she reveals the truth to the Druids—that she has betrayed them and borne the children of the enemy—and offers herself as the obligatory sacrificial victim necessary in rites of war. After a tender duet, "Qual cor tradisti" (What a heart you betrayed), Pollione remembers what a wonderful woman Norma has been, and they die together on the funeral pyre.

Like so many operas that are now repertory favorites, *Norma* was not successful at its premiere in 1831 at La Scala in Milan. The opera fared better soon afterward, however, and was staged dozens of times in Italy and elsewhere in Europe in the 1830s. Bellini attributed the lackluster premiere—which he described as a fiasco—to fatigued singers and a hostile audience; some of the spectators, he believed, may have been claques supporting a rival composer. Just as sports players are booed or distracted by fans of the opposing team, many composers faced aggressive rival detractors on opening nights. The tradition of booing lives on mostly in Europe, where the most vociferous booers are known as the *loggionisti*. They sit in the cheap seats at La Scala in Milan, are sometimes referred to as "hissing hooligans," and are feared for their hostility toward singers or directors who have displeased them. Alexander Pereira, the artistic director of La Scala, told *The*

Guardian in 2014 that many world-class singers refuse to perform at La Scala "because they are intimidated, if not frightened to death."

Gioachino Rossini, born in 1792 (the year after Mozart's death), certainly faced his share of noisy detractors. Gangs of vociferous "anti-Rossinistes," as they were known, booed the 1816 premiere of *Il barbiere di Siviglia* (*The Barber of Seville*), which, in addition to being marred by human catcalls, was interrupted by the meows of a real cat that had wandered onto the stage during Act I. But, like *Norma*, *Il barbiere* quickly recovered from the opening night difficulties.

The opera is based on Beaumarchais's *Le barbier de Séville*, the first in his trilogy of revolutionary-era Figaro plays, which had already inspired an opera buffa by the composer Giovanni Paisiello, whose supporters were irate that Rossini dared use the same material. Paisiello's version, which premiered in 1782, was popular in its day, but it has long been surpassed by Rossini's take on the story. As in Mozart's *Marriage of Figaro* (based on the second play in the Beaumarchais trilogy), there are myriad cases of mistaken identity in *Il barbiere di Siviglia*. Figaro, the barber of the title and the former servant of Count Almaviva, helps the Count woo and marry the pretty Rosina against the wishes of her lecherous old guardian, the creepy Dr. Bartolo. The Count wants Rosina to genuinely love him instead of just swooning over his power and wealth. In the first of several disguises, he impersonates a poor student called "Lindoro." To gain access to the house, the Count then pretends to be a soldier searching for lodging. In his third and final disguise, he impersonates a music teacher. The Count eventually marries Rosina, who becomes the mournful Countess Almaviva in Mozart's *Marriage of Figaro*.

Rossini's orchestration is more complex than Bellini's, and in the overture you'll hear an example of the Rossini crescendo. *Crescendo* is a common musical term that signifies a progressive increase in volume; its opposite is *diminuendo*, a term signifying a progressive decrease in volume. Rossini used the crescendo as a theatrical device, repeating a phrase with additional instruments and some harmonic changes to create a sense of excitement. The crescendo adds an ominous chill to Don Basilio's aria "La calunnia è un venticello" (Slander is a little breeze), which is about how rumors can quickly destroy an opponent. Don Basilio (Rosina's music teacher) is accompanied by an orchestral crescendo as he describes how the burbling noise of disinformation increases to fever pitch to ruin someone's reputation—in this case the Count's. Rossini also uses the crescendo to notable dramatic effect in the final section of Act I, a comic scene of mistaken identities and general pandemonium in which everyone is duped by the count, who is now in disguise as a billeted soldier. Figaro mocks the nonplussed Bartolo for standing frozen like a statue. The pace and volume quickly pick up as the voices of the Count, Figaro, Basilio, Bartolo, and Rosina form a dense, overlapping tapestry as they declare, in a crescendo of melodious confusion, that they feel bewildered and crazed. Recordings capture the musical beauty of such scenes, but the comedy is much funnier live, when the cast's facial expressions and physical gestures add to the merriment.

Figaro's Act I patter aria "Largo al factotum" (Make way for the handyman) is a sort of solo version of this riotous ensemble. In *patter arias*, which are common in opera buffa, a male character repeats words and spits out sentences with rapid-fire, tongue-twisting speed. Mozart used them in *The Marriage of Figaro* and *Don Giovanni*, and W. S. Gilbert and Arthur Sullivan (a librettist and composer, respectively) continued the tradition in songs like "I Am the Very Model of the Modern Major General," from *The Pirates of Penzance* (1880). They are the opposite of the flowing legato that begins bel canto arias such as Rosina's "Una voce poco fa" (A voice a while ago), a coloratura showpiece in which she declares her love for "Lindoro" and reveals her desire to outsmart her old guardian. Bel canto arias often feature two parts: a slow and expressive *cantabile* illuminating the character's emotions, perhaps sung as the character muses over a difficult situation, and a faster and more rhythmic *cabaletta*, which might reveal a contrasting side of his or her personality. While the cantabile is usually slower, it can also be highly ornamented, as in the first part of "Una voce poco fa."

The word "ornamentation" may imply something that has a purely decorative purpose, but in bel canto opera the ornaments have an important theatrical function and enhance the impact of the text. In this case the coloratura allows Rosina to express her passion for "Lindoro," and each time she sings "Lindoro mio sarà" (Lindoro shall be mine), the line is more elaborately ornamented. First she demurely sings that she is docile and respectful, but in the energetic and rhythmically forceful cabaletta she reveals the more cunning side of her personality.

Il barbiere is one of the era's comedic high points. Gaetano Donizetti also contributed plenty of laughs with *L'elisir d'amore* (*The Elixir of Love*), in which a dim-witted villager purchases what he thinks is a magic potion from a visiting charlatan in order to woo his love, and *Don Pasquale*, in which an amorous young couple outwits a lustful old man. Donizetti's personal life certainly often wasn't lighthearted, however. An overworked composer who was often worried about his finances, he suffered many tragedies: none of his three children survived infancy; his wife died after the birth of the third; and he contracted syphilis, had a mental breakdown, and was committed to an asylum in Paris. In addition to his brilliant comedies, Donizetti (who died in 1848 at age fifty) also wrote historical operas, including several works about the Tudor queens.

One of his most significant contributions is *Lucia di Lammermoor*, based on Sir Walter Scott's gothic novel *The Bride of Lammermoor*. Nineteenth-century artists found Scottish culture, history, and landscapes alluring, and Scott's story, about a deadly love affair between the children of enemy families, inspired several musical versions. In the opera the story unfolds in the late seventeenth century on the east coast of Scotland, where the Ashton family fortune is threatened by Edgardo of Ravenswood. Enrico Ashton wants his sister, Lucia, to secure a politically and financially advantageous marriage to Lord Arturo Bucklaw, but Lucia and Edgardo are secretly in love. The quintessential romantic opera (which, written in 1835, premiered shortly after Bellini had died and Rossini had retired), it was a hit, and was even mentioned in nineteenth-century novels, including *Anna Karenina*. Lucia's madness intrigued Victorian-era writers interested in how emotional crises could precipitate a woman's mental breakdown, or, in the parlance of the times, drive her to "hysteria."

A scene in Gustave Flaubert's novel *Madame Bovary* depicts the contrasting reactions of a dull husband, Charles, and his adulterous wife, Emma, during a performance of *Lucia di Lammermoor*. Like Lucia, Emma Bovary loves the "wrong" man, and both women are unhappy with the relationships prescribed to them by family and society. Emma is entranced by the passion on stage and experiences the opera on a purely visceral level, while Charles remains unmoved, and puzzled by the plot twists. Emma becomes irritated when he reminds her that he "likes to get things straight," and asks her to clarify the proceedings. Charles embodies the futility of trying to enjoy opera—which is often not a logical enterprise—on a purely cerebral level. But Emma has the right attitude: she "let herself be lulled by the melodies: she felt a vibration pass through her whole being, as if the bows of the violins were being drawn across her own nerves."

Flaubert describes the emotional impact on Emma of one particular scene: "Lucie was left alone, and the flute was heard like the murmur of a fountain or the warbling of birds. Lucie attacked her cavatina in G major bravely. She plained of love; she longed for wings. Emma, too, fleeing from life, would have liked to fly away in an embrace." The cavatina referred to is "Regnava nel silenzio" (Silence reigned)—in which Lucia recalls how she saw an apparition near the fountain, the ghost of a girl murdered by a jealous lover. The ornamentation in this aria highlights Lucia's mental instability: when she sings "e l'onda prìa sì limpida di sangue rosseggiò" (the clear water of the fountain pools turned red with blood), the coloratura reflects her distress.

In Act II, Lucia is duped and told that Edgardo has married another woman, and she reluctantly agrees to marry Arturo, but as she signs the marital certificate she is racked by foreboding. Her premonitions are proven right when Edgardo unexpectedly shows up. In the ensuing sextet, "Chi mi frena in tal momento" (Who restrains me at such a moment), the characters, beginning with Edgardo and Enrico, simultaneously express their reactions and emotions: Edgardo sings of his love for Lucia, Enrico his guilt. Raimondo (the chaplain), meanwhile, expresses his pity. Donizetti wrote different melodies for each soloist, and the bass, baritone, tenor, and soprano voices combine to beautiful effect. Lucia's despairing outbursts soar dramatically above the other voices.

Edgardo is distraught when he learns of Lucia's upcoming wedding to Arturo and declares he wants to die. In Act III, Lucia murders Arturo on their wedding night; still brandishing the bloody knife, she rants about her adored Edgardo. She reminisces about the sweet sound of his voice and hallucinates as she descends into the abyss of insanity. The flute part in this famous mad scene was originally written for glass harmonica, an instrument invented by Benjamin Franklin and built with different sizes of glass bowls. They produce an eerie sound when the rims are rubbed with a moist finger. The ghostly timbre vividly conveys the "celestial harmonies" that Lucia hears as she hallucinates a marriage to her beloved Edgardo. (These days you might hear either the harmonica or the flute used in the mad scene.) Neither Lucia nor Edgardo survives this miserable state of affairs: she collapses, and he commits suicide.

ROSSINI, LIKE DONIZETTI, DEMONSTRATED A REMARK-able gift for both comedy and tragedy. Beethoven, who was impressed with *The Barber of Seville*, had rather snarkily advised Rossini to stick to comedy, warning him that he would probably fail in weightier genres. But Beethoven was wrong: among Rossini's serious works (which include a version of Shakespeare's *Otello*) is his final opera, the masterpiece *Guillaume Tell* (*William Tell*), which heralded a pivotal moment in the evolution of the voice. Beethoven, incidentally, struggled to write opera. Mozart's genius proved adaptable to many different genres, but some of his Austrian and German successors, even those (like Franz Schubert and Robert Schumann) who were masterful song writers, struggled to write stage works. *Fidelio*, Beethoven's only opera (which premiered in 1805 and was revised several times after that), was inspired by the ideals of the French Revolution. It is an homage to bravery and resistance as well as an ode to marital love (which Beethoven never experienced). *Fidelio* is a prominent example of a genre known as *rescue operas*, which developed in France after the Revolution and featured stories about the liberation of the oppressed. While Beethoven's opera isn't as masterful as his most remarkable symphonies, piano sonatas, and chamber music, it does feature some gorgeous music and can make an impact in the theater.

Rossini had already written some three dozen operas when *Guillaume Tell* received its premiere in 1829 at the Paris Opera. It was his youthful swan song: Rossini retired as an opera composer at age thirty-seven and lived as a bon vivant, gourmand, and mentor while continuing to compose chamber music and a few large-scale vocal works. In addition to his operatic legacy, Rossini (who died in 1868) is remembered in culinary circles for the aptly named Tournedos Rossini—a dish of filet mignon, foie gras, and truffles.

The four-act opera is based on the play *William Tell* by Friedrich Von Schiller, an influential author in the German Romantic movement, who explored operatic themes of love and country and the dilemmas of those caught between the two. One highlight of the opera is Tell's poignant Act III aria "Sois immobile" (Remain motionless), which the titular hero (an archer who fought to free his country from the tyranny of Austrian occupation) sings after being ordered to shoot an apple off his son's head by the cruel Austrian governor. It opens with a mournful melody played by cellos that accompany Tell with yearning, hymnlike solemnity. The opera's overture is very recognizable—it was reincarnated as the theme to *The Lone Ranger* and has been featured in Disney movies and cartoons—as well as a sex scene in Stanley Kubrick's *A Clockwork Orange.*

In addition to his comedic gifts, Rossini could paint majestic natural scenes with his music. In the final scene of *Guillaume Tell*, when the exuberant citizens of a newly independent Switzerland celebrate their freedom, the music first depicts a storm on the lakeshore, then mellows to convey the clouds dissipating. A harp arpeggio ripples out in gentle waves as a sunny alpine melody unfolds in the horns and winds. The chorus and soloists sing an ode to liberty and to the magnificence of nature in a radiant, uplifting conclusion to the opera. *Guillaume Tell* was well received at its premiere and a critic rightly predicted that the performance heralded a new era. It proved an important step in the development of French grand opera, a genre that features large orchestras and choruses, dance elements, four or five acts, and librettos exploring serious themes of historical significance. Written between the late 1820s and the mid-nineteenth century, these works were often performed at the Paris Opera in lavish productions notable for pioneering staging elements. Some of Giacomo Meyerbeer's grand operas (including *Les Huguenots*—which depicts the bloodshed in sixteenth-century France between the Catholics and Protestants) were popular in their day, and though seldom staged in the twentieth century, are now being revived and recorded. Hector Berlioz's extravagant *Les Troyens* (*The Trojans*), based on Virgil's *Aeneid*, was infrequently staged until recent decades. It was beautifully recorded in 2017, with Joyce DiDonato singing the role of Dido, the Carthaginian queen.

Revivals of infrequently performed works offer opera buffs and new listeners the chance to hear something different from the so-called *standard repertory*, a core group of audience favorites like *Carmen*, *La bohème*, and *La traviata* that are frequently performed. In opera's earliest days, there was no such thing as a standard repertory—audiences wouldn't see different productions of the same opera, because works weren't intended to be restaged every season. Listeners demanded fresh new works, and composers churned them out: Handel wrote some forty operas and Donizetti almost seventy, for example, an unheard of number for a contemporary composer, for whom a single new opera now faces almost impossible pressure and scrutiny. Operas have fallen in and out of popularity over the centuries, and it's possible that the standard repertory might be quite different fifty years from now. Handel's operas, after all, were neglected for centuries.

Rossini's grand opera *Guillaume Tell*, which signified a pivotal moment in operatic history, was popular in its era but seldom performed in the latter part of the twentieth century. It has received a number of prominent productions in recent years, however, including, in 2016, its first staging at the Metropolitan Opera since 1931.

Rossini wrote the role of Arnold (a young Swiss revolutionary) for a tenor who sang with the light, agile voice then in vogue, and it was sung soon afterward by the French tenor Gilbert Duprez, who amazed audiences with the power of his voice. Instead of singing the high notes in his final aria in falsetto, he sang them with a chest voice, which rendered them much louder and more powerful than they would have been in falsetto. Audiences were thrilled with his resonating high C's, but Rossini compared the sound to that of a capon having its throat cut. Just as the orchestral instruments prevalent in opera's infancy sound different from their modern counterparts, the operatic voice has also evolved substantially since the seventeenth century. The new style of singing inaugurated by Duprez in *Guillaume Tell* paved the way for the dramatic tenor and dramatic baritone, voices with a weightier sound and darker timbre that featured prominently in late nineteenth-century operas.

While Rossini hated the sound of Duprez's high notes, he certainly would have been impressed if he had heard the Italian tenor Luciano Pavarotti sing high C's. Pavarotti, who died in 2007 at the age of seventy-one, wowed the cognoscenti and also brought opera to a mass audience. "The Three Tenors," a group that featured Pavarotti, Plácido Domingo, and José Carreras, sold millions of recordings. "Nessun dorma" (No one sleeps), an aria from Giacomo Puccini's *Turandot*, became a part of popular culture after Pavarotti sang it at the 1990 World Cup. Pavarotti, who was often criticized for his lack of physical acting skills, had an instantly recognizable voice and sang with a deep expressivity. He was nicknamed "King of the High C's" because of his ability to nail notes in a high register. Many arias requiring such a feat are from the bel canto operas, a specialty of Pavarotti's. In the aria "Pour mon âme" (For my soul) from Donizetti's comedic *La fille du régiment* (*The Daughter of the Regiment*), the love-struck Tonio sings nine high C's (which are an octave above middle C on the piano). Pavarotti was much admired for his performances of this aria, which helped propel him to stardom in the 1960s. When a singer makes it seem effortless and produces a pure, ringing sound on the high notes, the effect is thrilling. Singers often try to sustain these *money notes* (stratospherically high notes) for seemingly inhuman durations, driving their fans into a frenzy. Later in his career, however, Pavarotti was unable to hit the mark and transposed down to lower notes in live performance.

Omissions (or flubs) of the high notes can irk die-hard opera fans. In February 2017 at the Metropolitan Opera, the gifted Mexican tenor Javier Camarena was heckled by a listener during a performance of Bellini's *I puritani* (*The Puritans*) for omitting the high F in "Credeasi, misera" (The poor girl believed), although his overall performance in the opera was widely praised for its musicality, technical skill, and expressive depth. (A video featuring the high note in question, sung by the superb American tenor Lawrence Brownlee, currently one of the best bel canto interpreters, is posted on YouTube.) Although hearing a star sing high notes with such beautiful tone and seemingly effortless stamina is certainly a thrilling element of opera, fanatical outbursts from irate fans can reduce the art form to mere showmanship. Vittorio Grigòlo, an Italian lyric tenor admired for his beautiful voice and charismatic stage presence, described the pressure to hit the high notes in an interview in 2011 with *The Guardian*. "Opera is just like tennis or boxing or Formula 1," he said. "The critics moan that Federer's backhand is no good any more or that Nadal is too muscly, but do they know how to put the ball up there and really serve it? It is the same for tenors with the high C. If we fuck up that note in *La bohème*, we lose the whole opera. It is a dangerous profession, that is why people are so excited to hear us."

The soprano Maria Callas certainly drove fans into a frenzy, and her mystique and talent still captivate (and divide) opera fans. After hearing Giuditta Pasta (the soprano for whom he wrote the role of Norma) sing "Casta Diva" (Chaste Goddess), Bellini cried and said, "She sings and declaims in a way that draws forth tears....Even I wept... for all those many emotions I felt in my soul." It's certainly hard not to be moved when listening to Callas sing this aria. Callas, who died of a heart attack at age fifty-three in 1977, had a profound impact on the opera world. She was born in New York to Greek parents and had an unhappy childhood. Her tumultuous adulthood included a brief affair with the Greek shipping magnate Aristotle Onassis (who left her for Jacqueline Kennedy). Callas's distinctive voice wasn't conventionally beautiful, and her technique was fallible toward the end of her career, but her innate musicality and the sense of drama and emotional intensity she brought to roles captivated listeners. One of her many achievements was to help revive the bel canto repertory. Music that languished neglected or misunderstood was often brought to public attention centuries later only when a dedicated artist revealed its beauty. Bach's cello suites (composed circa 1720) were deemed dusty technical exercises not suitable for public performance until the cellist

Pablo Casals revealed their profundity in the early twentieth century. Bach's *Goldberg Variations* for keyboard were
similarly neglected until the pianist Glenn Gould captivated the public imagination with his interpretation in the
mid-twentieth century. And, as we'll see in an upcoming
chapter, opera conductors have also been an important
force in reviving the music of earlier eras.

Just as Casals played Bach's cello suites in a manner that demonstrated they were far more than boring
finger exercises, Callas revealed that the bel canto repertory was more substantive than critics, including the
nineteenth-century French composer Hector Berlioz, had
deemed to be. These critics had scorned the ornamentation
of bel canto as empty virtuosity and mere sensual pleasure,
perhaps because, when sung badly, the cascades of notes
sounded like birds chattering, leading some to deride it as
"tweety-bird" opera. Callas, who was an electrifying actress,
could not only handle the virtuosic requirements far more
skillfully than most of her predecessors, but demonstrated
how the ornamentation could propel the drama and illustrate a character's emotions and situation. In the mad scene
of *Lucia di Lammermoor*, the soprano can personalize the
music with her own ornamentation to illuminate the character's descent into madness. In a recording of Callas singing this role, she begins the scene with a chilling calm that
belies Lucia's desperate condition. When Lucia begins hal-
lucinating and implores Edgardo to take refuge at the foot
of the altar, Callas's use of ornamentation reflects the character's mental state. When she repeats the name "Edgardo"

at the end of the aria, Callas emphasizes the word with a desperate fervor: "Edgardo! Edgardo! Oh, me felice! Oh gioia che si sente, e non si dice!" (Edgar! Edgar! Oh, happy me! Oh, joy that I feel, and cannot express!). For comparison, listen to a recording of Joan Sutherland singing this same scene.

Like Callas, the soprano Sondra Radvanovsky has also elicited divided opinions from opera fans. Radvanovsky's voice has a dark, unusual timbre and is distinctive and highly expressive, although not a conventionally pretty voice. Radvanovsky has said she admires Callas because "she paid attention to the text and the music and was willing to make an ugly sound, if the text and music called for it." Indeed, some of the musicians best able to make an emotional connection with the audience, whether singers or instrumentalists, are the ones willing to take risks. Better an emotive, albeit slightly flawed, performance than a chilly and perfect one. Of course, the greater the risk a performer takes in a live performance, the higher the chance of a missed or harsh note, blemishes that can be erased in studio recordings as easily as a model's imperfections are Photoshopped. But while nobody wants to hear a consistently out-of-tune singer, airbrushed perfection shouldn't be the goal of a live performance—beautiful singing (and indeed, the most powerful music making) is always about much more than that.

In any event, notions of vocal beauty and operatic structure were soon to receive a stern challenge from a German composer named Richard Wagner, who had very different ideas about what constituted beautiful singing, and indeed, about almost everything else in opera. Wagner was a one-man revolution who turned much of the existing tradition upside down in his efforts to create what he deemed a perfect and complete work of art.

CHAPTER 3

GIANTS OF THE NINETEENTH CENTURY

ON WAGNER, VERDI, AND CONDUCTORS

RICHARD WAGNER HAS SURELY ELICITED A MORE OPER-
atic range of reactions from listeners than any other composer, from the adulation of fans who fly across the world
to see new productions of his operas to the hatred of those
who refuse to listen at all because of the racist ideology
he espoused. In between are the many who have been
entranced, fascinated, bored, or perplexed by his works—
perhaps all during the span of a single opera. Wagner, who
wrote his own librettos, believed that words and music were
equal, and broke new ground with his ideas about how opera should be experienced in the theater. He disparaged
the term "opera" and instead called his later works "music
dramas," believing Greek tragedy the ideal form of theater
and that opera should explore moral dilemmas. He aimed
to create what he called the *Gesamtkunstwerk*—which

translates as "total work of art." According to *Gesamt-kunstwerk* principles, artists should strive to reunite all the arts—music, poetry, dance, and visual arts—which he believed had become fragmented since the classical age. The influence of his music and ideas extends far beyond the nineteenth-century opera house to contemporary theater, cinema, and even nuptials. Did you know that the ubiquitous wedding staple "Here Comes the Bride" is an excerpt from a Wagner opera? His theories have also strongly influenced architecture.

Wagner, born in 1813 in Leipzig, was never sure of his paternity, an insecurity reflected in the recurring theme of missing or deceased parents in his operas. One of his early professional posts after a brief period of study at the Leipzig Conservatory was the music directorship of a theater in Riga, Latvia, where he moved with his wife, Minna. Wagner struggled throughout his life to manage his finances and fell into debt in Latvia, where the couple's passports were confiscated. They escaped their creditors by sneaking onto a ship bound for London, a dangerous journey that (according to Wagner) inspired *Der fliegende Hol-länder* (*The Flying Dutchman*), the story of a sailor doomed to sail the seas forever unless redeemed by the love of a faithful woman.

The theme of redemption is integral to Wagner's operas, along with the battle between good and evil, carnal and spiritual. In *Lohengrin*, based on a medieval epic poem, Wagner explored the limits of blind trust in a relationship between a knight in shining armor (named Lohengrin) and a damsel in distress (Elsa), who is unjustly accused of murdering her brother, Gottfried. The music of *Lohengrin* is sublime, its mystical interludes punctuated by militaristic fanfares evoking the tenth-century setting in warring Antwerp. Wagner described the events unfolding in the ethereal eight-minute prelude as such: "Out of the clear blue ether of the sky there seems to condense a wonderful, yet at first hardly perceptible vision; and out of this there emerges, ever more and more clearly, an angel host bearing in its midst the sacred Grail. As it approaches earth, it pours out exquisite odors, like streams of gold, ravishing the senses of the beholder."

When the violins play delicately in a high register to convey the idea of spiritual purity, the music certainly ravishes our senses. We hear those gorgeous shimmering violins soon afterward in Elsa's Narrative, in which she sings of how she prayed to be rescued by a knight who would prove her innocence, and again when the mysterious Lohengrin turns up in a boat led by a magic swan. Elsa and Lohengrin are to be wed on one condition: she agrees to never ask his name or origins. Anyone who has only heard "Here Comes the Bride" played on a keyboard at a wedding is in for a nice surprise: in the opera, a serene choir sings the melody, accompanied by rippling harp and woodwinds. It's ironic that the music has become a symbol of everlasting bliss, because this Wagnerian marriage is doomed. Just as Orfeo can't resist turning to check that Euridice is following him out of Hades (despite having been instructed not to do so), Elsa (quite understandably) can't restrain herself from inquiring about her husband's identity. The answer comes at a price: since she has not respected the protocol of anonymity required for all knights of the Holy Grail, Lohengrin must now disappear. Elsa dies of grief.

Love does triumph in Wagner's *Der Ring des Nibelungen* (*The Ring of the Nibelung*), although viewers must wait an awfully long time for that moment. Fans of J. R. R Tolkien's *Lord of the Rings* will already be familiar with some of the ideas at the core of Wagner's mammoth four-opera cycle. Both the opera and Tolkien's trilogy were inspired by Germanic and Norse myths, although Tolkien denied he was influenced by Wagner's masterpiece, claiming that "both rings were round, and there the resemblance ceases." (The first two novels of the trilogy were published in 1954, with the third following the next year; Wagner's cycle was first performed in entirety in 1876.) During the four operas of the Ring Cycle a complex story unfolds about the downfall of the gods and the triumph of love over greed, corruption, and power. Wagner, a German nationalist, began working on the Ring Cycle in Zurich, where he had fled to avoid arrest after participating in the uprisings of 1849 in Dresden. The monumental task of composing both the music and the text for the Ring—whose four works total about fifteen hours—took him about twenty-five years. He wrote the librettos in reverse order but set them to music in chronological order, thus working on the libretto for *Götterdämmerung* (*Twilight of the Gods*, the final installment in the cycle) some twenty years before composing the music.

Wagner's earlier operas, including *The Flying Dutchman* and *Lohengrin*, incorporated *leitmotifs*—musical themes that represent a character, place, emotion, or object and are repeated frequently throughout a particular work. Other composers had also used musical themes, but in the Ring Cycle Wagner used leitmotifs with particular sophistication. They resurface throughout the operas and are integral to his storytelling: they indicate when a particular character will appear, what the character is feeling, and the mood of the situation. Just as you know what's coming when you hear the famous theme in the movie *Jaws*, Wagner's leitmotifs function in part as a kind of musical signpost to the story. The way Wagner used these themes influenced many film composers, including Max Steiner (who wrote the soundtracks for *Gone with the Wind* in 1939 and *King Kong* in 1933). When told he had inaugurated the genre of modern film music, Steiner attributed that distinction to Wagner. John Williams composed several now instantly recognizable leitmotifs for the *Star Wars* series, including the triumphant tune played by the brass that begins each episode, the ominous march that heralds the arrival of Darth Vader, and the gentler motifs associated with Yoda and Princess Leia. Howard Shore used leitmotifs in his score for the cinematic *Lord of the Rings* film series starting in 2001, in which the heroic-sounding Fellowship motif and the pastoral, gentle Shire theme resurface.

The first opera in the Ring Cycle sets up the story of the omnipotent Ring, which Wotan (lord of the gods) needs to retain his power, although Erda (the goddess of nature and mother of his daughters) warns him that the Ring will hasten the gods' downfall. A prominent theme first heard in *Das Rheingold* (*The Rhinegold*) is the motif associated with Wotan, which represents the castle Valhalla and is played by Wagner tubas. Wagner invented these special tubas and had them built for the Ring Cycle; they produce an elegant, mellow timbre. In the prelude to *Das Rheingold*, the joyous-sounding nature theme is played by the horns and rises over the murky drone of the double basses. The theme—consisting of the notes of an E-flat major chord—is repeated slowly and expansively, swirling to an ecstatic climax that depicts the undulating waters of the Rhine River and the creation of the world. While other composers hinted at upcoming tragedies in their overtures, this prelude sounds triumphantly optimistic— foreshadowing not the corruption, greed, and sorrow soon to unfold, but the return to nature and the triumph of love.

In the first scene, the ugly Alberich (a Nibelung, or dwarf) becomes smitten with three beautiful Rhinemaidens, but they humiliate him. He learns about the Rhinegold and how anyone who forges a ring from the treasure will rule the world, but there's a catch: he must sacrifice love. Alberich readily curses love, steals the gold, and fashions a ring. Meanwhile, as payment for building a castle called Valhalla, Wotan has promised Freia (the goddess of youth) to the giants Fasolt and Fafner, who are depicted with a lumbering, heavy-footed motif. But without Freia, the gods will age and wither, so the giants are offered Alberich's treasure as alternative payment. Wotan steals the ring from Alberich, who curses it. Wotan's dalliances with Erda have produced nine warrior daughters called the Valkyries, who bring fallen soldiers from Earth to Valhalla. In fact, the association of opera with spear-carrying women wearing helmets came from this opera: the Valkyries—the feisty lady warriors of Norse mythology—were mostly depicted thus in early productions of the Ring Cycle.

In addition to the brood of Valkyries, Wotan fathers twins (Siegmund, a boy, and Sieglinde, a girl) with a mortal woman. The twins are separated as children and meet again in *Die Walküre* (*The Valkyrie*), the second installment in the cycle and the one most frequently performed as a standalone opera. In the prelude to Act I, the orchestra depicts a storm with electrifying intensity: the double basses and cellos play relentless crescendos and diminuendos to depict torrential rain, and the frantic tremolos in the upper strings evoke gusts of wind. When Siegmund takes shelter during the storm at the house of Sieglinde, who is now married to the brute Hunding, they don't recognize each other. Siegmund gazes at her in silence while a lone cello plays an almost unbearably tender melody. This is a love motif, one of many moments in Wagner's operas when music speaks louder than words. Their instant attraction isn't diminished when they discover they're related, and while this might seem more than a little creepy, Wagner's music indicates that it's a relationship of the utmost purity. The love motif is heard again in Siegmund's lyrical, soaring "Spring Song"—in which he describes the change of seasons and compares his love for Sieglinde to spring. Wagner uses the orchestra like a brilliant landscape painter to depict a thawing wintry landscape becoming lush and verdant again. Siegmund embraces Sieglinde as "bride and sister," but their bliss is short lived, and they are pursued by Hunding. Wotan orders his daughter Brünnhilde, the leader of the Valkyries, to protect the twins and ensure that

Siegmund defeats Hunding, but Wotan's long-suffering wife, Fricka, is horrified by this incestuous, adulterous affair and wants the twins punished.

Wotan submits to his wife's wishes and, in an emotionally turbulent monologue (which lasts some twenty-five minutes), he explains the whole messy situation to Brünnhilde and orders her to kill Siegmund, but she refuses. The most famous passage in *Walküre* is the "Ride of the Valkyries," which opens Act III as the Valkyries ride about shouting their battle cry ("Hojotojo!") and looking for fallen heroes to bring to Valhalla. The theme has been used in several films, including *Apocalypse Now* (1979), where it is blasted from a loudspeaker on the American helicopters as they attack a Vietnamese village.

Wotan is furious that Brünnhilde has disobeyed him and as punishment says he will turn her into a mortal woman; not only that, but she will slumber under a spell and marry the first man who stumbles upon her. The threat of withering in a humdrum marriage to a bossy mortal fills Brünnhilde with dread, and in a poignant duet with Wotan she negotiates a more palatable punishment: she will sleep in a ring of magic fire and marry the man heroic enough to brave the flames. *Walküre* concludes with the intoxicating Magic Fire Music. The brass instruments play the valiant theme associated with the hero who will rescue Brünnhilde, and the magic sleep motif is repeated with languorous insistence, eventually fading away to a celestial whisper as she falls into a deep slumber.

In the penultimate installment of the Ring, Wagner introduces Siegfried (the son of Siegmund and Sieglinde), whom Wotan hopes will save the gods. But the young man, at first brutish and immature, is about to be undone himself—by love. He finds Brünnhilde asleep on the mountain—incidentally, his first glimpse of a woman—and is emotionally shattered. In stark contrast to the testosterone-driven music of Act I, the final scene opens with music of blissful tenderness as Siegfried evolves from an invincible meathead to a vulnerable young man who has learned the meaning of fear. In *Götterdämmerung*, the final installment in the cycle, Siegfried gives the Ring to Brünnhilde as a symbol of his faithfulness, but after being drugged with a magic potion, he quickly forgets about her, marries another woman, and is murdered. "Siegfried's Funeral March," often played as a standalone piece at symphonic concerts, begins with a faint drumbeat and swells to a triumphant march as the vassals carry away his body. During the Immolation Scene, Brünnhilde rides her horse into Siegfried's funeral pyre, Valhalla is consumed in flames, and the Rhinemaidens take back the Ring. The rule of the power-hungry gods is over and a new age of man has begun, but while the gods may have been felled, this is music of the divine.

The Ring Cycle might sound exhausting, and attending a performance after a long day at the office may not sound appealing. But in Wagner's day no one went to the opera after sitting at a desk all day. He wanted his audience to savor the music as an immersive experience, so he built a theater specially for his Ring Cycle in the German town of Bayreuth. It was funded by King Ludwig II of Bavaria, who had a huge crush on the womanizing Wagner (who did not return his affections). Instead of mimicking the ornate glamor of other European opera houses, Wagner modeled his theater on a Greek amphitheater and opted for simple decor and spartan seating. It heralded a new way of experiencing opera: the house lights were dimmed, meaning that since the audience was sitting in the dark, they actually had to concentrate on the performance instead of socializing, as had long been the norm. (Such decorum became the norm much later in Austria and Italy.) Wagner built a special pit so the musicians were out of view of the audience. The complete Ring Cycle was performed for the first time in 1876 at Bayreuth, which continues to host the annual Bayreuth Festival. Mark Twain, who visited Bayreuth in the 1890s, described the experience as making him feel like "a sane person in a community of the mad."

WAGNER TOOK A BREAK FROM WORKING ON THE RING Cycle to write *Tristan und Isolde*—an opera about an overwhelming passion that can only be consummated in death. He was smitten at the time with a young woman named Mathilde Wesendonck, who was married to one of his patrons. *Tristan* was scheduled to receive its premiere in late 1862 in Vienna, but even after dozens of rehearsals the orchestra musicians and singers couldn't navigate Wagner's score. It fared no better after fruitless rehearsals in various other European cities, but eventually received its premiere in 1865. *Tristan* is based on a medieval Celtic legend about a knight, Tristan, who drinks a magic potion and falls in love with the Irish princess Isolde, who has drunk the same potion. But she is inconveniently betrothed to Tristan's uncle and employer, the elderly King Marke of Cornwall. After their illicit love is discovered, Tristan is stabbed by a knight loyal to the king, and after a long third act, dies in Isolde's arms. While carnal desire symbolizes their earthly passion, only after death can their two souls be united and their longings satisfied. Shortly before beginning to compose the opera, Wagner had read works by Arthur Schopenhauer, who believed that ambition, hate, love, and sexual desire were more powerful than the intellect. Schopenhauer, unlike Wagner, didn't believe that music and poetry were equal, and considered music the most exalted art form. His influence on Wagner is clear, however, in *Die Walküre* and *Tristan*, operas in which the orchestra often seems to be the most powerful narrator. After reading Schopenhauer, Wagner said he had found "a sedative" that helped him sleep at night: "It is the sincere and heartfelt yearning for death: total unconsciousness, complete annihilation, the end of all dreams—the only ultimate redemption."

Wagner wrote music of R-rated sensuality in *Tristan*. Clara Schumann (a composer and the wife of the nineteenth-century composer Robert Schumann) described the music as "disgusting," writing in her diary that she resented having to "see and hear such crazy lovemaking the whole evening, in which every feeling of decency is violated." Nineteenth-century critics had certainly tut-tutted about the immorality of *Carmen* and *La traviata*—but they were mostly decrying the degeneracy of the characters, not the music itself. So what kind of music could possibly have seemed so debauched to nineteenth-century listeners? In polite society, chords were expected to behave a certain way. Wagner challenged established decorum with the "Tristan chord," which makes a rebellious appearance in the opera's opening measures. While writing *Tristan*, Wagner had begun to tinker with the established harmonic system of tonality in radical new ways.

Tonal music is based on major or minor key scales. On the piano there are twelve notes from middle C to the C above it: seven white keys and five black keys. Each scale has seven different notes and starts and ends on the same note: the eight notes together are called an octave. The tone C is the tonic or tonal center of a piece in C major, for example, and in general, pieces in a major key sound cheery and those in a minor key sound more melancholic. Tonal music often features hummable tunes and ends in the tonic key. (If you play "Happy Birthday" in C major and end with a C minor chord, you'll alarm the partygoers.) In the tonal system, dissonant chords invariably resolve to consonant chords, providing a feeling of closure and resolution, but the "Tristan chord" leads immediately to another dissonant chord. Since ambiguous endings are invariably more unnerving than tidy harmonic resolutions, this evokes an unsettled feeling. Wagner prolonged the chord's yearning sense of incompletion until the final moments of the five-hour opera, whose "outrageous discords" startled some early listeners. To our twenty-first-century ears, the dissonances sound quite mild-mannered compared to some genres of rock or heavy metal, but it's still easy to understand why a prim nineteenth-century listener might have been scandalized. The unresolved chord leads to music that surges with an animalistic drive, its unhinged yearnings sounding primordial, and yes, almost indecent. After its goose-bump-inducing first incarnation in the opening measures of the prelude, the Tristan chord resurfaces throughout the opera, the longing almost resolved in Act II. The lovers have met in secret to consummate their passion but are interrupted by King Marke: the music surges forward, longing for resolution, but is abruptly thwarted. It's a well-known passage of musical coitus interruptus.

The tension finally dissipates in opera's most spine-tingling climax—the intoxicating finale of Isolde's "Liebestod" (Love-Death), or transfiguration. The theme of an eternal love consummated in or after death was common in nineteenth-century literature and painting. When Isolde sings the "Liebestod," Tristan has died, and she is in a trance-like state as she gazes at him. She hallucinates that he is calling her to another realm before she sinks, unconscious, onto his body in a mystical union. Perhaps Clara Schumann was blushing as she listened to the orchestra swell to ecstatic heights and the yearning Tristan chord finally resolve in orgiastic bliss.

Unlike in the Ring Cycle, with its many narrative twists and detours, there's not much of a plot in *Tristan*; instead, Wagner explores the inner worlds and psychological journeys of the two lovers. *Tristan* is a contemplative, meditative work, and listening to it requires a completely different state of mind than listening to a work by Mozart, Rossini, or even some of Wagner's other operas. Go with the flow—let yourself be subsumed and consumed by the journey, and if it still feels long, know that you're not alone. Listeners have long protested the length of Wagner's operas: after attending the first complete Ring Cycle at Bayreuth, Tchaikovsky compared leaving the theater after *Götterdämmerung* to being released from prison. Wagner described his style, with its unresolved phrases and continuous flow, as "endless melody," but to some it just felt, well, endless. Rossini famously quipped that Wagner had beautiful moments but bad quarters of an hour. He wasn't wrong.

Compared to the momentum of the instrumental music, Wagner's lengthy monologues and duets can indeed seem static, occasionally interminable. You're unlikely to come away humming the melody of a Wagnerian monologue, because instead of setting words to a memorable tune, like his predecessors and contemporaries did, he wrote in a more declamatory vocal style. But after a slow stretch, an exhilarating conclusion like that of *Tristan* seems even more intoxicating and cathartic. In any event, feeling bored during a Wagner opera, unlike performing in one, has never proven fatal—in 1911 and 1968, two conductors suffered heart attacks while conducting the second act of *Tristan*.

In an interview in 2015 with the *Daily Telegraph*, when asked why the mammoth Ring Cycle still attracts devoted fans, the conductor Antonio Pappano said, "You can lose yourself in it. And we need that in our lives, that feeling of being lost." He's entirely right: think of experiencing the Ring as binge-watching a Netflix series featuring an eclectic group of characters whose struggles and passions are illustrated with some of the most radiant music ever composed.

Wagner, a megalomaniac, wrote glorious music, but he was an odious person who championed a racist ideology. He wrote several important essays about music, including "Opera and Drama" and "The Artwork of the Future," as well as a virulently anti-Semitic pamphlet called "Judaism in Music." Wagner believed that German art had become degenerate and was nothing more than bourgeois capitalist entertainment. He blamed the Jews for ruining German art and insulted even the Jewish composers who had helped him professionally, such as Giacomo Meyerbeer. The Nazis often played Wagner's music at their events and quoted his racist statements in their propaganda. Performing Wagner in Israel (where the operas have never been staged) has been taboo since the founding of the Jewish state, and listeners have protested the inclusion of his music in live orchestral concerts, although his works are sometimes broadcast on public radio. The Israeli-Argentine conductor Daniel Barenboim (who is Jewish) has challenged the taboo by performing Wagner in concert, sometimes to heated opposition: some audience members heckled him with shouts of "fascist" during a concert in Jerusalem in 2001 that featured an excerpt from *Tristan and Isolde*. In 2017, the Australian director Barrie Kosky became the first Jewish director to work at the Bayreuth Festival, staging Wagner's *Die Meistersinger von Nürnberg* (*The Master-singers of Nuremberg*), one of Hitler's favorite operas. In the opera, which Wagner set in sixteenth-century Nuremberg, the Meistersingers— who are also craftsmen of various trades—hold a song competition whose winner will marry a beautiful young woman called Eva. In a final monologue, the cobbler-poet Hans Sachs warns of the threat of "foreign ways" and extols "holy German art." In Kosky's staging, Sachs is depicted as Wagner himself, speaking the words from the witness stand in the courtroom of the Nuremberg Trials.

In addition to the difficulties of staging Wagner, there are the difficulties of singing Wagner. Performing Wagner presents a different set of challenges from performing bel canto repertory, for example. The operatic voice has evolved along with other elements of the genre. Monteverdi and his colleagues wrote for small ensembles with instruments that produced softer sounds than their modern counterparts. You'll struggle to hear a viola da gamba (a baroque cousin of the modern cello) in a large concert hall, for example. In the eighteenth century, violins had gut strings, which produced an earthier tone and less resonant sound than the steel strings of modern instruments. (But while they didn't need to project over large, powerful orchestras, singers did need to compete with the sounds of chattering audiences!) Wagner wrote for larger and louder orchestras, and singers need stamina to sing for the extended periods required. In opera there is no "magic ring" of amplification to help them project over orchestras that create dense thickets of sound. Along with sheer vocal heft, the best Wagnerian singers also possess a beautiful timbre.

Birgit Nilsson, a Swedish soprano who died in 2005 at the age of eighty-seven, was one such singer. She grew up in southern Sweden on a farm, which her father wanted her, his only child, to manage. But instead of becoming a farmer, she attended a music conservatory in Stockholm and became one of the great Wagnerians, particularly admired for her interpretation of Isolde and Brünnhilde. Nilsson had remarkable stamina and sang with seemingly effortless freshness even after a long evening, when other singers might start to sound tired. She could project her deeply expressive voice over a huge orchestra without sounding forced or shrill. She nailed her high notes and, thanks to her excellent breath control, could hold them for an impressively long time. The beauty of her voice can still be enjoyed on recordings, although the experience of hearing her live at her prime was said to be incomparable. "It was the almost physical presence of her shimmering sound that made it so distinctive," wrote Anthony Tommasini in 2006 in the *New York Times*. "You had to have heard the voice live to know how it shone—like a laser, straight and unfailingly true," according to Edward Seckerson's assessment in *The Independent*. Indeed, hearing a great singer live is a visceral experience quite different from the experience of listening via recording.

During some of Nilsson's performances of *Tristan and Isolde*, she sang with the Canadian tenor Jon Vickers as Tristan. Like Nilsson, Vickers (who died in 2015 at the age of eighty-eight) worked on a farm and sang in local church choirs during his youth. Tenors who sing Wagnerian roles such as Tristan are called *heldentenors* (heroic tenors): they have large, clarion voices and the endurance to sing vocally exhausting parts. The Danish tenor Lauritz Melchior (who died in 1973 at age eighty-two) sang Tristan at the Metropolitan Opera 128 times: during his prime he impressed audiences with the heft and musicality of his voice and set a benchmark for future performers.

OPERA HAS BEEN A FREQUENT TARGET OF SATIRE—AND Wagner has certainly received his fair share. On YouTube there are videos of the British comedian and singer Anna Russell (who died in 2006) doing her summation of the Ring Cycle, a parody complete with musical demonstrations of the various leitmotifs on the piano. After discussing some particularly fantastical incident or character in her deadpan voice, she interjects with "I'm not making this up, you know!" She describes Wotan as a "crashing bore" and the Valkyries as "noisy." But, as Russell says, "That's the beauty of Grand Opera, you can do anything as long as you sing it." And as for the conclusion of *Götterdämmerung*? "You're exactly where you started twenty hours ago!"

The Viennese composer Oscar Straus spoofed the Ring Cycle in his 1904 operetta *Die lustigen Nibelungen* (*The Merry Niebelungs*). Warner Brothers mocked Wagner in the 1957 cartoon "What's Opera, Doc?," in which Elmer Fudd (dressed like Siegfried) sings "Kill the Wabbit" to the tune of the "Ride of the Valkyries," and Brünnhilde (Bugs Bunny in drag) sports a horned helmet. Such a helmet, incidentally, having vanished from the opera stage many decades ago, remains one of the most stubbornly enduring stereotypes about the art form, despite the fact that horned helmets are now about as common on the opera stage as typewriters are in the office.

Some of these parodies have been duly savaged as sacrilegious, but people have been making fun of opera for centuries. Visual artists in early eighteenth-century London mocked Italian opera with engravings that depicted the castrati as grotesquely misshapen. The English ballad operas, satirical works that blended popular tunes and dialogue, also took aim. *The Beggar's Opera*—by the theater impresario and librettist John Gay—satirizes (among other targets, including the British legal system) the "unnatural" conventions of opera seria and the flamboyance of the castrati. It was a huge hit at its premiere in London in 1728, appealing to local audiences looking for accessible entertainment in their own language.

There was also a tradition in the late nineteenth century of operatic parody. Jacques Offenbach is best known for his final work, the lavish *Tales of Hoffmann*—a macabre grand opera about a poet who recalls his unhappy love affairs with a mechanical doll, a consumptive soprano, and a courtesan. But before writing this sinister swan song (which he hoped would cement his reputation as a "serious" composer), Offenbach had spent most of his career writing *operettas*. This genre features song and spoken dialogue and was the precursor of the contemporary American musicals. Operettas, like musicals, provided both lighthearted entertainment and a platform to explore social and political issues. One of Offenbach's best-known operettas is *Orphée aux enfers* (*Orpheus in the Underworld*), whose overture and finale includes the cancan. Offenbach parodied the mythical story of Orpheus: in his version, Orpheus and Eurydice hate each other, and when Eurydice is bitten by the snake, she happily goes to the underworld to be with her lover, Pluto. Orpheus is glad to be rid of her, but a character called "Public Opinion" admonishes him that he must rescue her. As well as bashing revered elements of Greek mythology and classical drama, Offenbach also parodies music from Gluck's version of the story. In England, the Victorian-era duo Gilbert and Sullivan produced a large catalog of operettas in which they lampooned politics, the British class system, and opera itself. Many of their works are still frequently performed today, including *The Pirates of Penzance* and *The Mikado*.

Wagner's legacy extends not only to opera, theater, and literature (as well as providing ample fodder for satirists), but to the role of the conductor. As orchestras expanded from small baroque ensembles to mighty Wagnerian armies, singers needed more powerful voices, and a conductor was required to marshal the amassed forces into a cohesive group. During performances of choral music in the Renaissance, a time-beater might use his hand or a roll of papers to indicate tempo for the singers: the earliest conductors were concerned more with logistics than nuance. Wagner, himself a conductor, had revolutionary ideas about the role of the conductor, who he felt should act not merely as a traffic warden but also as an interpreter. Baroque orchestras were chamber ensembles, small groups in which the composer often played the continuo part and guided the ensemble from the harpsichord, which was placed amid the other musicians. The keyboard player would give cues and, when not playing, use his hands to direct the proceedings. Handel conducted his operas from the keyboard in this manner. In eighteenth-century ensembles, the first violinist (also known as the concertmaster) was often a co-conductor. During performances by period-instrument ensembles today the harpsichordist or concertmaster often plays and conducts in this manner.

The first orchestras were certainly of varying quality. Leopold Mozart was impressed by one ensemble he and Wolfgang heard in 1763 in Mannheim, Germany, noting in a letter that it consisted "altogether of people who are young and of good character, not drunkards, gamblers, or dissolute fellows." The role of the musician-conductor in these early ensembles was more organizational than creative: the main goal was to ensure that everyone was playing in sync and in tune. The role of the conductor evolved significantly in the nineteenth century: instead of performing alongside other musicians and conducting from an instrument, the conductor directed the ensemble from a podium. In operas with large casts and choruses, the maestro must still act as a traffic warden and ensure that entrances and balances are correct, but the job entails far more than that. The conductor shapes the artistic interpretation, and his or her decisions regarding tempo, dynamics, phrasing, and other nuances can dramatically alter how a particular piece sounds.

Tempo, for example, is a crucial (but very subjective) interpretative decision. Composers write markings like "allegro" (fast) or "adagio" (slow) in the score to guide the performer, but each tempo marking spans a small range. If an opera conductor chooses a tempo that is too slow, the pacing might be dramatically inert; if the tempo is too fast, the singers might sound rushed and breathless. The chosen tempo can have a profound effect on the emotional impact of a particular piece of music, as the same singer can make a very different impression when singing an aria at a markedly slower or faster pace. In addition to deciding on tempo, the conductor might need to choose between different published editions of an opera and decide what (if any) cuts to make. The conductor will also interpret the composer's dynamic markings, because, just as with tempo, there is no one objective definition of "forte" (loud) or "piano" (soft). One conductor might choose to highlight a crescendo with unusual vigor or play a phrase in an unusual way for special effects. Some conductors interpret judiciously, while others like to make more extreme statements, sometimes to the detriment of the music. The conductor must be familiar with every element of the opera, since he or she will work with the singers, orchestra, and staging director.

Some conductors use a baton to keep time, while others carve the air with their bare hands. Whereas during a symphony concert the conductor is visible on a podium, in a traditional opera house the orchestra performs in a pit. (In more off-the-beaten-track venues, the orchestra might be visible to the audience.) The conductor also communicates with the musicians via facial expressions and other physical movements. Some conductors are reserved and use minimal hand gestures or precise baton movements, while others leap around and gesticulate wildly.

Just as the efforts of Maria Callas and Joan Sutherland spurred the revival of bel canto opera, conductors have been a vital link to formerly neglected repertory. Callas elevated the status of bel canto music when she demonstrated how to wield the ornamentation to dramatic and emotive purpose. Similarly, conductors in the late twentieth century who specialized in baroque repertory brought substantial insights to operas by Handel. Baroque music as presented in historical recordings conducted by Wilhelm Furtwängler (1886–1954) or Herbert von Karajan (1908–1989) is almost unrecognizable when compared to interpretations by early music specialists. Furtwängler's tempos are so ponderous that the notes sound as if they're being dragged through treacle, and the luxuriant string-playing that sounds so glorious in Wagner's music (a specialty of both Karajan and Furtwängler) overwhelms early music, which requires a more transparent sound. In a 1950 recording of *Giulio Cesare* conducted by Hans Schmidt-Isserstedt, the overture lasts almost six minutes—twice as long as in most modern performances. When played at this extremely slow pace, the overture suggests an interminable evening ahead. Pacing is a crucial element of conducting opera. Of course, we'll never know exactly how the music sounded in the baroque era. But in versions today conducted by Marc Minkowski, Emmanuelle Haïm, William Christie, or Nikolaus Harnoncourt, the *Giulio Cesare* overture sounds buoyant, crisp, and alive, and, importantly, it builds excitement for the drama to come.

An Italian conductor, Angelo Mariani, was almost arrested in 1847 when the Austrian authorities decided that his interpretation of Giuseppe Verdi's *Nabucco* (*Nebuchadnezzar*), a biblical story about oppressed peoples that was a hit at the premiere in 1842, was so feisty that it could have incited nationalistic Italians to revolt. (Presumably, if Mariani had conducted a more lethargic rendition, the officials wouldn't have been so concerned.) Verdi was a leading figure in the Risorgimento, the midcentury movement for Italian independence, and the Chorus of the Hebrew Slaves, "Va, pensiero" (Hasten, thought), from the opera became a symbol of Italian nationalism. Verdi, a perfectionist, often fretted that most conductors didn't interpret his scores correctly, but he approved of Arturo Toscanini (1867–1957), one of the first celebrity conductors. Toscanini, who loathed the rowdy audiences at La Scala, was a remarkable musician, but he was also a tyrant, setting a precedent for the stereotype of the strong-willed conductor with an iron baton. Toscanini led the orchestras and choirs singing "Va, pensiero" at Verdi's funeral in 1901, an event attended by huge crowds.

When the conductor Daniel Barenboim opened the 2013 season at La Scala in Milan with Wagner's *Lohengrin* instead of a Verdi opera, it was as if he had decided to wear the colors of a rival sports team: the locals weren't pleased, and the Italian press declared it an insult to national pride.

WAGNER AND VERDI, BOTH BORN IN 1813, HAVE BEEN pitted against each other in posterity like boxers vying for a trophy of aesthetic dominance. In 2013, in honor of the bicentennial of their births, fans staked out claims to greatness for both composers. The Royal Opera hosted a Verdi versus Wagner debate in London, and experts were asked to opine in various newspaper columns about the relative merits of each composer. Verdi and Wagner never actually met in person, and Verdi was irate when someone dared suggest he had been influenced by Wagner. In light of their strikingly different aesthetics, any given individual may feel a greater affinity with one composer or the other, but fortunately, we have plenty of opportunities to enjoy the music of both of these geniuses without having to choose between them.

There's no doubt that Verdi is now the more popular composer: according to Operabase.com, *La traviata* (*The Fallen Woman*) was the most performed opera worldwide between the 2011–2012 and 2015–2016 seasons, receiving a whopping 4,190 performances. Only one of Wagner's operas makes the site's list of the 25 most popular operas in those years: *The Flying Dutchman*, which clocks in at no. 24, received 957 performances during the period. Verdi was also unquestionably the better person: a man whose death was mourned by a nation. But moral integrity often has little relevance to an artist's posthumous popularity. So why is Verdi still the most frequently performed opera composer worldwide? For the same reasons he was always popular: his vocal writing is gorgeously tuneful and his operas full of irresistible melodies. Whereas Wagner's operas, inspired by mythology and philosophy, feature gods, magic potions, and fantastical creatures, Verdi chose stories based on historical figures and events and focusing on human relationships, which he depicted with remarkable insight. He loved Shakespeare, whose plays inspired three of his twenty-eight operas: *Otello*, *Macbeth*, and *Falstaff* (his final opera, and only successful comedy).

La traviata was one of the first operas by an Italian composer to deal with topical issues like prostitution and disease. The fallen woman with a heart of gold was a popular character in nineteenth-century literature, but the censors certainly weren't pleased with the subject matter for Verdi's opera, based on Alexandre Dumas's play *La dame aux Camélias* (*The Lady with the Camellias*), a romanticized depiction of Dumas's affair with a real-life courtesan. Along with censoring blasphemy and unflattering portrayals of authority figures, the moral guardians of opera also curtailed subject matter deemed licentious. Verdi wanted to highlight the topical relevance of the issues explored in *La traviata* but was forced to set the opera in the early eighteenth century instead.

Verdi had been born in the Parma region of northern Italy, the son of an innkeeper who encouraged his early musical training. As an adult he had an unconventional lifestyle, cohabiting in Paris with a soprano, whom he eventually married, named Giuseppina Strepponi. She was ostracized when they moved back to Italy. Their living arrangements—rebellious for the era—perhaps informed *La traviata*, the story of a passionate love affair between the courtesan Violetta Valéry and Alfredo Germont, a "respectable" gentleman whose family prospects are threatened by his illicit romance.

Consumption (now called tuberculosis) killed many people in nineteenth-century Europe, with the poet John Keats, the Brontë sisters, and Chopin among its victims.

The disease was sometimes romanticized by artists and writers, and consumption fells quite a few nineteenth-century heroines, including Violetta. The premiere of *La traviata* was a fiasco, in part because the audience deemed the soprano portraying Violetta to be too old and portly for the role of a beautiful young consumptive. In our time, the opera inspired the Baz Luhrmann film *Moulin Rouge!*, starring Nicole Kidman, as well as the movie *Pretty Woman*, during which the escort played by Julia Roberts is moved to tears when taken to see *La traviata*.

In the prelude to the opera, the violins play a melody that sounds both urgent and fragile as it unfolds like a soprano's gentle lament. This shimmering leitmotif alludes to Violetta's impending death, and when it resurfaces later during the opera it reminds us of her ephemeral existence. But Act I opens on a festive note, with Violetta and the partygoers toasting the pleasures of hedonism during the *brindisi* (a drinking song). Alfredo (Violetta's admirer) declares his love for her in "Un dì, felice, eterea" (One day, happy and ethereal), but she insists she cannot love him back. Just as Mozart illustrated the contrasting personalities of Donna Anna and Don Ottavio, Verdi reveals the characteristics of each protagonist: Alfredo's sincere words unfold in long, sensual lines gently accompanied by the orchestra, while Violetta's callous rebuttals are revealed in flighty coloratura outbursts.

But she soon reveals a more introspective side. In public she is a vivacious party girl, but privately she mourns the emptiness of her life. "È strano! È strano!" (It's strange, it's strange), she softly muses, contemplating whether Alfredo

could be The One, before suddenly abandoning what seems
like the crazy notion of settling down. In an ode to hedonism, "Sempre libera" (Always free), she sings that she will
always be free, the joyous orchestral music reflecting her
newly carefree mood. She soon succumbs to domesticity,
however, and moves in with Alfredo, but Giorgio Germont
(his father) worries that their scandalous cohabitation will
jeopardize his daughter's impending marriage. Germont
persuades Violetta to leave Alfredo but feels remorseful,
knowing that Violetta is a kind-hearted woman. The forlorn melody from the prelude sounds even more melancholy when repeated before Act III. In the heartbreaking
final scene, Violetta bids farewell to the past in "Addio, del
passato," her soaring lines now unornamented, the coloratura whirlwinds of her party-girl persona replaced with
music of poignant solemnity. "È strano!" (How strange),
she sings, musing how odd it is that she no longer feels any
pain. In a brief burst of euphoria, she declares that she will
live, but the turbulent orchestral music indicates otherwise.
Violetta succumbs to consumption.

Verdi, who became a widower at age twenty-seven, also
lost his two young children in quick succession to illness.
He was so distraught by the trio of deaths that he struggled
to complete a commission for a comic opera and nearly
abandoned his fledgling opera career. And yet he pressed
on and wrote *Nabucco*, one of several operas in which he
explores familial dynamics. His five-act grand opera *Don
Carlo* depicts a love triangle that includes a father and
son, while father-daughter relationships are at the heart
of *Simon Boccanegra* and *Rigoletto*, Verdi's second most

frequently performed opera and one in which he expanded the vocal and dramatic scope of the baritone role. Rigoletto, a court jester, is a psychologically complex character who elicits both our distaste and our pity, and who, like Violetta, has a public and a private persona. In private, Rigoletto is a loving father who dotes on his own daughter, Gilda. In public, he is the sneering sidekick of the lascivious Duke of Mantua, he enjoys taunting Count Monterone, who is upset because the Duke has seduced his daughter. The Count takes revenge by declaring a curse—"La maledizione!"— on Rigoletto. In the prelude, the brass instruments play an ominous motif that is used later to depict the terrible curse that destroys the title character. After an encounter with an assassin, Sparafucile, Rigoletto compares his life as a court comedian with the murderer's role in an introspective soliloquy, "Pari siamo!" (We are equal). We are two of a kind, observes Rigoletto:

> *My weapon is my tongue—and his*
> *the dagger;*
> *I make the people laugh, he makes*
> *them mourn!*

The opera was inspired by Victor Hugo's 1832 play *Le roi s'amuse* (*The King Amuses Himself*), about a lecherous early sixteenth-century French monarch and his corrupt and deformed jester. *Rigoletto* was initially banned because the censors deemed it both immoral and trivial, but Verdi and his librettist, Francesco Maria Piave, made changes to appease the Austrian censors. (Venice at the time was under Austrian rule.) Verdi's melodic genius flowered in *Rigoletto*—whose tunes became the pop hits of his day. In the opening scene, the innocuously cheery music of "Questa o quella" (This one or that one) contrasts with the misogynistic words: the Duke declares that women are all the same to him and that he will never be faithful. The Duke's Act 3 aria "La donna è mobile" (Women are fickle) is equally sinister in content but equally hummable, so catchy, in fact, that Verdi put an embargo on it before the premiere—instructing the musicians not to hum it in public before curtain time. The tune did indeed prove irresistible and became a favorite of both the gondoliers of Venice and soccer fans throughout Europe. In "Caro nome" (Dearest name), Gilda's coloratura showpiece, she muses over the name of her beloved, a poor student called Gualtier Maldè, who is actually the Duke in disguise. While in the baroque and bel canto era both men and women sang highly florid parts, by Verdi's era such music had become restricted to female roles. This was partly logistical, because the male voices that could project over larger, louder orchestras with powerful brass sections tended to be heavier and less agile.

After Gilda is seduced by the Duke, Rigoletto swears revenge. In the quartet "Bella figlia dell'amore" (Beautiful daughter of love), the vengeful Rigoletto and the despairing Gilda watch from outside a tavern as the licentious Duke cavorts with Maddalena, his newest conquest (and Sparafucile's sister). The four voices—soprano, contralto, tenor, and baritone—reflect the character and emotions of the different protagonists. The Duke's music is flowing and sensual as he flirts with Maddalena, his seductive melody contrasting with Rigoletto's gruff declarations. Maddalena's music sounds flighty, Gilda's despairing. When Victor Hugo saw the opera in 1857 he marveled at this particular advantage opera has over spoken drama: "If I could only make four characters in my plays speak at the same time, and have the audience grasp the words and the sentiments, I would obtain the very same effect." In the final act, Verdi vividly depicts a storm, with the ominous string surges and cymbal crashes conveying howling winds and thunder. Rigoletto hires Sparafucile to assassinate the Duke and place his body in a sack, but Gilda sacrifices herself to save him. Rigoletto, who presumes the Duke dead, is then horrified to hear his voice from afar, singing "La donna è mobile." Rigoletto opens the sack and discovers that his beloved daughter is the one dying. The opera ends with Rigoletto's anguished cry of "La maledizione!"

A father-daughter relationship is also an important component of *Aida*, a success at both its premiere at the opening of the Cairo Opera House in 1871 and its European premiere the following year at La Scala. Verdi capitalized on the nineteenth-century Egyptology craze that began in 1798 after Napoleon invaded Egypt (where he was eventually defeated) and cartographers, scholars, and artists began to bring Egyptian stories, images, and artifacts back to Europe. *Aida*, based on a fictional story of ancient Egypt by the French Egyptologist Auguste Mariette, features a love triangle and explores the classic operatic dilemma of romantic love versus patriotic loyalty.

Verdi had never visited Egypt, but he researched ancient Egyptian instruments and went to great lengths to convey local ambience. While the music in *Aida* is of course not authentically Egyptian, Verdi's use of harmony is colorful and evocative and indicates that the story is clearly not taking place in nineteenth-century London or Rome. The banks of the Nile are depicted with sinuous woodwind melodies, and the haunting, melismatic vocal lines sung by the priestesses contrast with the somber, un-ornamented bass lines of the priests. As in *La traviata*, the prelude of *Aida* features a theme played on the high strings that represents the title character, an Ethiopian princess who is the daughter of the Ethiopian king Amonasro. She has been captured by the Egyptians and is in love with the high-ranking Egyptian soldier Radamès, who secretly adores her but will be betrothed to Amneris, the daughter of the Egyptian pharaoh.

Characters in opera are frequently feeling guilty about something. In this case, Aida, in love with an enemy of her people, suffers from Norma's conundrum. In the Act I "Ritorna vincitor" (Return victorious), Aida expresses the guilt she harbors about her illicit feelings for Radamès; after anxiously urging him to military victory, she becomes despairing when imploring the gods for pity. "Numi, pietà" (Gods, have pity), she sings, the violins framing her words with a tender sympathy. In contrast to such introspective moments are the magnificent choruses of Act II. Accompanied by brass fanfares and percussion, the populace and priests celebrate the victorious returning Egyptian army and sing patriotic odes, such as "Gloria all'Egitto" (Glory to Egypt). Following this is the famous Triumphal March, a scene that is occasionally staged with live elephants.

Guilt becomes too much for the homesick Aida in Act III, however, and her reverie about her homeland, in "O patria mia" (Oh my homeland), is interrupted by music that indicates she's in trouble with Amonasro. In a turbulent duet, he manipulates her into betraying Radamès. Amonasro softly sings that he knows about the illicit romance, and hints that Aida's lover might have useful information that could help the Ethiopian army. Aida lashes back in anguish, refusing this ruse, her cries underlined with percussive vigor in the orchestra. Fine, then, Amonasro basically says, telling Aida that after the Egyptians rape and pillage the Ethiopians, she will be blamed. She begs her father for pity, but Amonasro doesn't stop there, bringing Aida's dead mother into the picture to curse her disloyal daughter. After this fiery exchange, poor Aida, disowned, again softly begs for mercy, assuring her father she will choose loyalty to country over love. She tricks Radamès into revealing the route the Egyptian army will take, and he is then denounced as a traitor and condemned to be buried alive. He doesn't die alone, however, because Aida has snuck into the tomb to perish with him. In "O terra, addio" (Oh earth, farewell), the star-crossed lovers bid farewell to the world, their haunting duet interwoven with the sound of Amneris praying for his peace.

Against the grand opera backdrop of *Aida*—with its rousing choruses, dramatic orchestral marches, and elements of spectacle—the intimacy of such a moment is all the more striking. Verdi's human characters are worlds apart from Wagner's mythological protagonists, but with remarkable skill both composers movingly depicted the turmoil of romantic and familial relationships, creating intimate, finely etched scenes within large-scale works. The intricacies of parent-child relationships are not a focus in *verismo*, however, in which the drama revolves around turbulent love affairs. And instead of the gods, royals, and courtesans who take center stage in operas by Verdi and Wagner, humble folk—soldiers, villagers, and gypsies—are the stars of verismo. In this salt-of-the-earth and violent genre, philosophizing and introspection are replaced with raw, brutal, and deadly passions.

CHAPTER 4

REALISM IN AN UNREALISTIC MEDIUM

ON VERISMO, PUCCINI, AND SLAVIC OPERA

OPERA, WHOSE GENESIS WAS PROPELLED BY THE ARTIFICE of the castrato voice, is certainly an artificial art form on some levels. Even in works that feature human characters and real-life issues, there's invariably a moment when you have to suspend disbelief to accept plot twists such as two people failing to recognize each other in silly disguises. Since opera is so inherently unrealistic, it might seem strange to describe a particular genre as *verismo*—the Italian word for "realism"—which stems from the word *vero* (true). But as Handel's Alcina revealed, however illusory the situation, her feelings were real, and in verismo feelings are on steroids. Verismo opera grew out of a French and Italian literary movement in which writers like Émile Zola and Giovanni Verga depicted the often brutal aspects of life in humble social spheres. In verismo operas, there are no complicated mythological plots or heavy symbolism, and fewer aristocrats in sight. Instead, humble folk are featured in stories that are sensational and often lurid and often end with a crime of passion. Verismo is a soap-opera snapshot of human nature at its most elemental.

Just a few years after Verdi created the powerful mezzo-soprano role of Amneris, the French composer Georges Bizet capitalized on the sensual, dusky qualities of the mezzo-soprano voice to create the title heroine of his opera *Carmen*. Like Violetta, the gypsy temptress Carmen challenges societal norms. She's a free-spirited, independent woman who would rather control her destiny than submit to a man—even knowing her decision will bring her downfall. Carmen is now an iconic figure—a symbol of female sexuality, freedom, and desire.

The opera was inspired by Prosper Mérimée's 1845 novella of the same name and received its premiere at the Opéra Comique, a theater in Paris that had a reputation for family-friendly fare. Instead of monumental "grand operas" based on serious topics, the theater offered shorter, more lighthearted works, with morally sound stories that ended happily after the bad guys were vanquished. *Opéra comique* is also a genre, one which includes both arias and spoken dialogue. It stemmed from the early eighteenth-century tradition of vaudeville, but by the late nineteenth century the term was being applied to works that combined the spoken word and music, but weren't necessarily comedies. (So don't be confused if you hear the tragic *Carmen* referred to as opéra comique.)

An opera that featured a law-breaking seductress and ended with a murder certainly challenged the theater's

G-rated template. Management wasn't happy. Bizet, a depressive who had suffered earlier failures in the theater, was devastated by the scathing reviews from Parisian critics. While the press (who denounced the work as "undramatic" and "contemptible") and much of the public were duly scandalized by the opera's risqué story line, others enthused about the sensual music and powerful drama. *Carmen* received some forty-five subsequent performances that year and went on to be performed (to acclaim) in myriad European and American cities in the following years. Bizet was not able to enjoy the opera's success: he died at the age of thirty-six, three months after *Carmen*'s 1875 premiere, following a severe bout of rheumatism and two heart attacks.

The gorgeous music of *Carmen* reflects the influence of Bizet's mentor, the composer Charles Gounod, whose works include a sensually scored *Roméo et Juliette* based on the play by Shakespeare. In addition to *Carmen*, Bizet is remembered for his youthful *Les pêcheurs de perles* (*The Pearl Fishers*), about a priestess heroine facing a dilemma between secular love and her sacred vows. The opera's popular duet "Au fond du temple saint" (At the back of the holy temple) is often sung as a standalone excerpt. But *Carmen* is Bizet's best seller, a work whose earthy realism is a stark contrast to the storyline of *The Pearl Fishers*.

Carmen, a precursor of verismo, takes place around 1830 in Seville, a city seen by many composers as a sensual and "exotic" place. (*Fidelio*, *Don Giovanni*, and of course *The Barber of Seville* are among the Seville-based operas.) Bizet had never visited Andalusia, but he went to great lengths to source genuine Spanish melodies and to create music that sounded authentically Spanish, just as Verdi worked hard to create an "authentic" ambience for *Aida*. The local Spanish flavor is evident right from the opening notes of the lively prelude, which is interwoven with the jaunty tune of the Toreador Song and Carmen's five-note "fate" motif. Both sensual and ominous, this exotic-sounding motif resurfaces at key moments, including after the Habanera, "L'amour est un oiseau rebelle" (Love is a rebellious bird)—Carmen's seductive entrance aria—in which she touts the fickleness of love amid a crowd of factory girls and their young military admirers. The opening words, "Love is a rebellious bird / that no one can tame," descend with slinky, luxuriant insouciance.

Interpreting a character like Carmen requires a voice that conveys the character's sensuality, as well as a charismatic stage presence. One of the most convincing interpretations in recent years has been that of the Latvian soprano Elīna Garanča, who delivered a performance so physically seductive and fiercely raw that it was easy to understand how the upstanding soldier Don José couldn't resist her. She sang the role in a 2010 Live in HD performance in Richard Eyre's production at the Metropolitan Opera, and her interpretation of the Habanera is available on YouTube (an upload that at time of publication had received more than seven million views). A production from 1980 at the Paris Opera relies more on castanet clichés, but the lustrous voice of the Spanish soprano Teresa Berganza conveys Carmen's flirtatiousness and sensuality, although Berganza is a less physical performer than Garanča.

The courtesan Violetta can never be "respectable," but she is still "nice"—her good-hearted qualities are extolled

by Giorgio Germont, and our sympathy is elicited through
Verdi's music. Carmen, on the other hand, certainly doesn't
have a heart of gold, but Bizet's music renders her irresistible. She embarks on a deadly affair with Don José, who
at first plays hard to get and declares that he will marry
Micaëla (a sweet-natured girl from his village). When he
reminisces about his childhood, the purity of the music
evokes both Micaëla's innocence and an idyllic village life.
It sounds a world apart from Carmen's rhythmically sultry
music, with its underlying current of danger. After Carmen
is arrested for stabbing another girl in a fight, Don José is
entrusted to guard her, but lets her escape. In Act 2, Carmen mocks him for being more beholden to roll-call than
love. Carmen drives Don José nuts: in the Flower Song,
Bizet charts his evolution from upstanding soldier to love-
struck psycho in musical terms as succinct as the notes in
a therapist's chart. Don José deserts the army. But freedom
proves less than intoxicating, and Carmen abandons him
for the champion bullfighter Escamillo. Don José implores
Carmen to return to him, but she is resolute: she was born
free and will die free. In a jealous rage, Don José murders
her. Fragments of the chirpy Toreador Song add a surreal
element to the swirling, passionate music of this scene. As
Escamillo emerges victorious from a bullfight, Bizet juxta-
poses the bullfighter's song with a final, defiant rendering
of the fate motif.

Such a bloody ending is typical of verismo. A prime
example of Italian verismo is the double-bill often referred to as "Cav-Pag," the abbreviated name for two short
operas: Pietro Mascagni's *Cavalleria rusticana* (*Rustic*

Chivalry) and Ruggiero Leoncavallo's *Pagliacci* (*Clowns*). The first was inspired by a short story by the Sicilian author Giovanni Verga about infidelity and revenge among Sicilian villagers; the second, in which life imitates art, is an equally lusty crime-of-passion opera set as a play within a play. In the prologue to *Pagliacci*, Tonio the clown addresses the audience directly:

> *Here on the stage you shall behold*
> *us, in human fashion,*
> *And see the sad fruits of love and*
> *passion!*
> *Hearts that weep and languish,*
> *cries of rage and anguish,*
> *And bitter laughter.*

The actor Canio, part of a traveling stage troupe, has discovered that his wife, Nedda, is having an affair. But the show must go on: he must put on his makeup and portray a clown called Pagliaccio who is betrayed by his wife, Columbina (enacted by Nedda). Canio, unable to mask his true emotions, has a very real meltdown and kills Nedda on stage, leaving his audience unaware that they've just witnessed a real-life murder. In the aria "Vesti la Giubba" (Put on your costume), Canio sings, "On with the motley, the paint and the powder": in other words, he will do his duty and entertain the audience despite his distress.

The aria heralded two milestones in operatic and cultural history. A recording with piano made in 1902 by the Italian tenor Enrico Caruso (1873–1921) in Milan became the first record to sell more than a million copies, according to *The Guinness Book of World Records*, and when Caruso sang the aria at the Metropolitan Opera in 1910 it was transmitted in the world's first public radio broadcast. Caruso was born poor in Naples and during his childhood sang in churches. He was distressed when a local claque booed him during a youthful performance in his hometown as punishment for his failure to pay them the requisite bribe, and declared that he would never again perform in Naples. Local foes proved a minor hazard compared to what he would later face in New York, however, where a terror and extortion racket called the Black Hand, composed of Italian immigrants, threatened to assault him if he didn't pay their bribe. Caruso went on to sing some three dozen roles with the Metropolitan Opera, performing more than 850 times with the company in New York and on tour. His prolific recordings helped him attain superstar status among an economically diverse group of fans. The sensual and burnished sound of his voice, albeit blemished by the irreversible crackle of old recordings, can still be heard in the many recordings he made between 1902 and his death.

Almost a century after Caruso's pioneering radio broadcast at the Met, the house was at the vanguard of another major technological innovation, a brainchild of general manager Peter Gelb. On December 30, 2006, a live performance of Mozart's *Magic Flute* was broadcast to cinemas around the United States and Britain, Norway, and Japan. The Live in HD series has since been expanded to other countries in Europe, South America, and Asia, and the Royal Opera in London also offers broadcasts. Popcorn and live opera are no longer strange bedfellows. While film audiences of course lose the thrill of hearing singers live in the theater, the broadcasts offer close-ups of the action that can certainly enhance the theatrical experience. Whether or not these broadcasts have been successful in ushering new audiences into actual opera houses is open to debate, but they have undoubtedly provided yet another way to enjoy opera. Caruso, whose career was propelled by his own recordings, would surely have been happy to have his performances beamed live into cinemas as well.

CARUSO SANG MANY ROLES BY PUCCINI, A MASTER MELO-dist who concluded the legacy of popular Italian opera that had begun with Monteverdi. Three of his operas, *Tosca*, *La bohème* (*Bohemian Life*), and *Madama Butterfly* (*Madame Butterfly*), were among the ten operas performed most frequently worldwide between the 2011–2012 and 2015–2016 seasons, according to Operabase.com. But despite being perennial audience favorites, Puccini's operas have been criticized for being little more than unsophisticated thrillers with emotionally manipulative scores. The British composer Benjamin Britten wrote that he was "sickened by the cheapness and emptiness" of *La bohème's* music, and in his 1956 book "Opera as Drama" the American musicologist Joseph Kerman famously called *Tosca* a "shabby little shocker." But there's a reason that Puccini's most popular operas have outlived such snark: the plots are straightforward, the drama is fast-paced, and the music is gorgeous.

"Chi ha vissuto per amore, per amore si morì" (He who has lived for love, has died for love) is the theme of Puccini's *Il tabarro* (*The Cloak*), a one-act potboiler about a cuckolded bargeman who takes revenge on his unfaithful young wife by killing her lover and hiding the body under his cape. Living and dying for love (and lust) were themes of both Puccini's operas and his own personal life, which was filled with scandals that seemed fodder for a verismo opera. One of nine children, and born in 1858 to an important musical family in Tuscany, Puccini became one of Italy's biggest musical stars but remained prone to self-doubt and depression. He worked as an organist in local churches before deciding (after seeing a performance of *Aida* in 1876) to try his hand at opera. He enrolled in the Milan Conservatory, and his first opera received its premiere in 1884.

Early in his career Puccini began an affair with a married woman named Elvira Gemignani, whose unfaithful husband was killed by the jealous spouse of one of his conquests. Puccini eventually married Elvira, with whom he had had a son out of wedlock, but continued philandering. Elvira became suspicious that he was having an affair with one of the maids, who committed suicide after being unfairly accused by Elvira. (Suicide is a fate that befalls several Puccini heroines.)

Puccini, like Mozart, was picky about his librettos, but with Giuseppe Giacosa and Luigi Illica he formed a collaboration as fruitful as the Mozart–Da Ponte union. The three Italians worked together on *La bohème*, *Tosca*, and *Madama Butterfly*. Having experienced penury while a student at the Milan Conservatory, Puccini could certainly relate to the young Parisians of *La bohème* (1896), a timeless story of young love inspired by a book by the French author Henri Murger, who had himself been a struggling young writer in Paris. These patronless French bohemians are like trust-fund-less artists everywhere: they suffer genuine poverty while mocking the establishment and making art. The story of the bohemians has been retold many times, including in the 1990s Broadway rock musical *Rent*, which updated the setting to the then grungy Lower East Side of Manhattan and changed the menace of tuberculosis to HIV. The consumptive seamstress Mimì, the poet Rodolfo, the painter Marcello, the singer Musetta, the philosopher Colline, and the musician Schaunard are the amiable protagonists of *La bohème*, and even the elderly landlord demanding his rent is genial (and easily manipulated with drink). Poverty is the only real villain in the opera, which opens with a quartet of witty bohemians freezing in their garret on Christmas Eve. When Rodolfo is left alone, the fragile Mimì arrives to borrow a match, then faints. In Rodolfo's tender aria "Che gelida manina" (How cold your little hand is), he introduces himself to Mimì as poor in material goods but "a millionaire in spirit," adding that "sometimes my strong-box / is robbed of all its jewels / by two thieves: a pair of pretty eyes." To twenty-first-century ears this might seem like a cheesy pick-up line, but when accompanied by such optimistic, innocent-sounding music it comes across as utterly genuine, wooing the sweet-natured Mimì and generations of Puccini fans.

In a gentle aria called "Mi chiamano Mimì" (They call me Mimì), she tells Rodolfo about her life as a loner and dreamer, and he admires her beautiful face, illuminated by moonlight. In the duet "O, soave fanciulla" (Oh, lovely girl), they celebrate their passion, their voices soaring above the swooning caresses of the string instruments. "Amor! Amor! Amor!" (Love! Love! Love!), the lovers sing as they exit the stage, the lush romanticism of the music contrasting with the threadbare settings. So why would critics like the composer Benjamin Britten, a twentieth-century genius, decry such music as cheap and empty? On the one hand, composers often bash each other's works: Puccini, for example, publicly criticized the music of Richard Strauss's *Salome*. In a letter to his wife in 1903, the composer Gustav Mahler derided *Tosca* as "a masterly piece of trash," noting that "nowadays, any bungler orchestrates to perfection."

Puccini certainly had an impressive gift for orchestration, and his richly textured music vividly complements the text. Listen to the way Puccini depicts the wintry scene outside a tavern on the outskirts of Paris at the opening of Act III, when a delicate, descending phrase played by harp and flute evokes a light snowfall. After unfairly accusing Mimì of being a flirt, which he knows she is not, Rodolfo confesses to Marcello that he is in fact afraid she is dying. "Mimì è tanto malata!" (Mimì is terribly ill!), he sings in a monotone over funereal chords, his plaintive despair turning to agitation that is echoed by soaring orchestral music as he admits that he can't provide any basic comforts for her. The voice of the innocent and fragile Mimì, who is listening to this exchange, unseen to the boys, interjects mournfully as she questions her own fate, a destiny that is soon unequivocal. The music is sophisticated, even if the way it tugs on our heartstrings is not subtle. In Act IV, back in the garret, she is dying. Since there is no heat or food, Musetta decides to pawn her jewelry and Colline his overcoat. Colline sings a tender farewell aria, "Vecchia zimarra" (Faithful old garment) to his trusty coat, and there's not a hint of sarcasm in this innocent and moving ode to an inanimate object. Left alone, Mimì and Rodolfo reminisce about their first meeting, and she soon quietly passes away. The opera ends with Rodolfo's anguished cry of "Mimì! Mimì! Mimì!"

After the tear-jerking *La bohème*, Puccini wrote a thriller called *Tosca*, in which the title character, who is very different from the delicate Mimì, gets the last word. *La bohème* is among the most realistic operas ever composed. Its themes concerning struggling young artists and illness are timeless—any poor artist without health insurance can relate to them still today. *Tosca* is more typical verismo melodrama, however, a story of lust, politics, betrayal, and murder starring a volatile opera singer (Tosca), her artist lover (Cavaradossi), and a sadistic police chief (Baron Scarpia). Puccini had been instantly smitten with the story after seeing Victorien Sardou's French-language play *La Tosca*, set at the time of the Napoleonic Wars, and wrote to his publisher asking them to secure rights. The opera received mixed reviews from critics but was a box-office hit after its premiere in Rome in 1900. Verdi and Bizet had worked diligently to create "authentic" sound worlds to convey the settings of *Aida* and *Carmen* even though they'd never visited Egypt or Seville, but Puccini actually visited Rome before writing *Tosca* to pick up details about the rhythms of the city. He learned at what hour church bells were rung and how they sounded, for example, from the Castel Sant'Angelo, one of three authentic Roman locations featured in the opera. He asked local acquaintances to confirm musical details about the plainchant melodies sung in Roman churches, and the precise pitch of the bells of St. Peter's.

The ominous opening leitmotif of dramatic chords is associated with Scarpia and heard whenever he enters the scene, or even when another character thinks about him. Unlike Verdi's multidimensional characters, Puccini's villain is unequivocally evil. So is Don Giovanni, but Mozart's music implies that he's at least a charming jerk. Puccini makes it clear that Scarpia has no redeeming qualities, accompanying him with sinister music like rumbling lower strings and growling bassoons.

The story begins in the church of Sant'Andrea della Valle, where the political prisoner Angelotti has just sought refuge. Cavaradossi is working on a painting of Mary Magdalene that is inspired by a beautiful woman he has seen praying at the church (the blue-eyed Marchesa Attavanti). In "Recondita armonia" (Strange Harmony), he contemplates the differences between the fair Marchesa and his dark-eyed Tosca and declares that even while painting another he thinks only of Tosca, who believes him to be unfaithful. Scarpia convinces Tosca that Cavaradossi is indeed unfaithful and tells the Sacristan to prepare for the Te Deum, the hymn of praise. "Tosca, you make me forget

God!" sings Scarpia at the end of a scene in which Puccini brilliantly blends devotion and depravity, the music of a religious procession swelling with ecstatic fervor as Scarpia's lustful outcries punctuate the sounds of the chorus, bells, and organ.

While Scarpia embodies pure evil, Tosca represents the romantic ideal that "He who has lived for love, has died for love." In Act II, Scarpia orders Cavaradossi to be tortured in earshot of Tosca, who laments her situation in the aria "Vissi d'arte" (I lived for art). The words "I lived for art, I lived for love," are paired with a sequence of four descending notes that unfold with a sense of dejection that reflects her state of mind. She has never hurt a living creature in her life, and she has always been a faithful woman: her despair rises to an anguished crescendo of grief as she asks why God has forsaken her in her hour of need. When Scarpia approaches Tosca and tries to assault her, she stabs him in the chest, killing him. "This is the kiss of Tosca!" she retorts. In Act III, Cavaradossi (who is in prison) sings of his love for Tosca in the aria "E lucevan le stelle" (And the stars shone), but they are not to be reunited: Cavaradossi is executed by Scarpia's firing squad, and Tosca commits suicide by throwing herself off a parapet.

As you've certainly noticed by now, operatic heroines often meet a predictable fate: they kill themselves after being driven to despair by a man, they are murdered by a jealous lover, or they die of consumption. In the best-case scenario, they end up in a convent. In the preface to her book *Opera, or the Undoing of Women* (1979), the French feminist philosopher and cultural critic Catherine Clément writes that "on the opera stage women perpetually sing their eternal undoing. The emotion is never more poignant than at the moment when the voice is lifted to die. Look at these heroines. With their voices they flap their wings, their arms writhe, and then there they are, dead, on the ground." On the one hand, Clément makes an irrefutable point: opera heroines frequently end up dead, the victims of male violence. But on the other hand, at least on stage their voices are heard loud and clear, unlike in real life.

Several recent op-eds published by the *New York Times* have discussed why women stay silent during company meetings. One, published in 2015 and titled "Speaking While Female," by Facebook CEO Sheryl Sandberg and Adam Grant, a professor at the Wharton School, described what happened when two women writers for a hit TV series tried to pitch ideas in a meeting. "Almost every time they started to speak, they were interrupted or shot down before finishing their pitch," they wrote. "When one had a good idea, a male writer would jump in and run with it before she could complete her thought." But if the article had been titled "Singing While Female," it would have had a very different slant. Unlike women fighting to be heard in a real-life public sphere, women hold the floor on the opera stage. They are given an uninterrupted chance to express their feelings and opinions in a way that the contemporary woman desperately trying to be heard in a boardroom meeting might only envy.

Opera has also offered women a rare avenue to financial success at times when they couldn't even vote or own property. The female divas who sang Handel's operas in London, for example, earned vast sums. It's also important to remember that opera, like all art, is a product of the cultural and political era in which it is created. Many operas have been based on mythology, poems, plays, and novels. Nineteenth-century opera often featured the fragile heroines and fallen women prevalent in literature of the era. While male characters in opera may have a higher survival rate, they're certainly often not exactly portrayed in a rosy light—we meet an endless crew of jealous psychos, womanizers, boorish jerks, murderers, and boring good guys. Sometimes the women sing the more powerful music: in *Don Giovanni*, neither Ottavio's mild-mannered tunes nor the title character's arias are as stirring as the music sung by Donna Anna and Donna Elvira. Men certainly don't hog the best roles in opera, and female singers are not discarded at a certain age like Hollywood actresses or television presenters. Indeed, on the opera stage, a middle-aged singer can perform the role of a teenager.

Puccini's *Madama Butterfly*, whose premiere in 1904 at La Scala was a fiasco, features yet another operatic cad and his victim, who commits suicide. Of all of Puccini's tragic heroines, the story of the Japanese geisha Cio-Cio San is perhaps the most heart-wrenching. Japan had signed trade treaties with several Western nations in the mid-nineteenth century, and there was significant interest in Japanese arts and culture, with exhibitions at the London Exposition of 1862, the Paris Exposition of 1867, and the Japanese

Pavilion at the 1867 Philadelphia Centennial Exhibition. Japanese traditions have inspired a number of Western artists, including Edgar Degas, Vincent van Gogh, Claude Monet, and Henri de Toulouse-Lautrec, as well as many poets and other writers. "Madame Butterfly" was the title of a short story by the American author John Luther Long, published in 1898, which in turn was influenced by a semi-autobiographical novel published the previous year called *Madame Chrysanthème*, by the French writer and naval officer Pierre Loti, which depicted a marriage to a "temporary wife." These works inspired a play by David Belasco that Puccini saw in London in 1900, *Madame Butterfly: A Tragedy of Japan*, which then inspired his opera.

The opera is set in Nagasaki in the early twentieth century, when a young US Navy lieutenant, Benjamin Franklin Pinkerton, enters a "temporary marriage" with a teenage geisha named Cio-Cio San (Madama Butterfly), who gives birth to his son (Sorrow). Since he had never visited Japan, Puccini researched its music, incorporating transcriptions of Japanese melodies and Japanese gongs in *Madama Butterfly*. He re-created the sounds of traditional Japanese instruments by using the flute, bells, and harp. Puccini depicts Cio-Cio San with the "exotic" sound of the pentatonic scale (which has five notes instead of the seven of the Western classical scale) and represents Pinkerton with a more "American" sound. A quote from "The Star Spangled Banner" opens his aria "Dovunque al mondo" (Throughout the world), in which he reveals how a traveling Yankee enjoys taking profit and pleasure with little thought for the consequences. This "easy going creed," as the American consul Sharpless describes it, is illustrated with a genial melody, despite its caddish content, just as Verdi sets the lecherous words of the Duke's "Questa o quella" (This one or that one) to a jaunty tune. Pinkerton is bewitched by Cio-Cio San's charms, observing that she is delicate and fragile: "Light as a feather she flutters / And, like a butterfly, hovers and settles, / with so much charm and such seductive graces," he sings. He adds that he is overcome with desire even though he knows he might damage her "fragile wings." Cio-Cio San is in love, although she apprehensively observes that in her husband's country butterflies are caught and stuck on a board with a pin. In the long, rapturous duet "Viene la sera" (Night is falling), they admire the night sky, and the languid, rapturous music conveys both their ardor and the radiance of twinkling stars.

Butterfly, initially innocent and optimistic, has renounced her ancestral faith, but she has substituted it with a naïve faith in human nature: in the exquisitely beautiful aria "Un bel dì" (One beautiful day), she sings of how one day she will be reunited with Pinkerton. When after three years she finally sees his ship on the horizon, she sets up a vigil to wait for him. Act II concludes with what is known as the *humming chorus*—an ethereal, wordless chorus tinged with sadness.

But Pinkerton has returned with his American wife (Kate) to take Sorrow to America. Pinkerton is not a Scarpia-like villain: when he realizes that Cio-Cio San has waited faithfully for him, he is full of remorse. In the devastating finale, we hear a quotation from a Japanese folk song. Butterfly reads the transcription on her father's knife: "To die with honor / When one can no longer live with honor." She bids her son farewell, blindfolds him, and commits suicide. After the crash of a gong, and the sound of the brass and string instruments in full force, we hear Pinkerton's anguished cry of "Butterfly! Butterfly! Butterfly!"

In addition to the misogynist elements of opera, there is also the question of how to address the racial stereotypes of characters such as Cio-Cio San, who serves as a plaything for a Western man. Puccini himself described her as a "dear little woman, fragile and beloved like a Japanese doll, without pretensions." In 2017, an entrepreneurial New York company called Heartbeat Opera, one of a number of "indie" companies that have sprung up in recent years in various cities, offered a production of *Madama Butterfly* that tried to deal with some of these stereotypes. The company trimmed the work substantially, reorchestrated the music for chamber ensemble, and framed the narrative with the silent figure of a young Asian American boy observing the story. One of the music directors, Jacob Ashworth, told the *New York Times* that the various revisions (which included omitting Act I) were an attempt to "tip the scales a bit, to take the romance out of its mythical setting and watch Cio-Cio San make her choice as a contemporary woman would." In this staging it was unclear whether she committed suicide or not. According to the director, Ethan Heard, "There's something fetishistic even about seeing that Japanese act of suicide, where audiences are wowed by the act of falling on a samurai sword." He emphasized that *Madama Butterfly* is a masterpiece, and that he and his team wanted to "honor the beautiful writing and score, but inject some questioning into it, and bring people in closer proximity to it."

And why not? It can be refreshing to see such thoughtful reinterpretations, which are certainly more valid than some of the outlandish concepts seen at mainstream opera houses. Heartbeat Opera recruited Asian singers for the roles of Cio-Cio San and her maid, an important statement in a production that aimed to challenge established perceptions of a particular character. There are occasionally valid reasons to cast according to race, as Heartbeat did, although, for the most part, opera companies have (or at least should have) color-blind casting policies, meaning that a white soprano can portray the Ethiopian princess Aida and a black soprano can sing Cio-Cio San. There's nothing particularly "authentic" about any of these roles in any event. Cio-Cio San is the creation of Italians who had never visited Japan, and who were inspired by a play by an American of Portuguese Jewish origin, who in turn had been inspired by a short story by an American writer and a novel by a French writer.

IN CONTRAST TO THE JAPANESE CULTURE FILTERED through Western eyes in *Madama Butterfly*, Leoš Janáček's *Jenůfa* was an authentically local product, based on a play by Gabriela Preissová, a Czech dramatist who grew up in the Moravian countryside. Her play, inspired by real-life events, was praised for its honest depiction of rural customs, but critiqued for its shocking themes of violence and infanticide. It was all a bit much for some commentators, who didn't want to acknowledge the possibility of such horrors occurring among their countrymen. Janáček, who was fifty when he completed *Jenůfa*, was born poor in 1854 in rural Moravia, the son of a village music teacher. Janáček studied regional folk music, and his transcriptions of spoken dialects influenced the vocal lines of *Jenůfa*, which reflect the rhythms and inflections of quotidian speech. (Janáček called this "speech melody.") His son died as a toddler, and his beloved twenty-year-old daughter, Olga, died as he was still writing the opera, which took him ten years to complete. "I would bind Jenůfa with the black ribbon of the long illness, the pain, and the sighing of my daughter Olga and my little boy Vladimir," he wrote in his autobiography decades later. Janáček had seen and enjoyed Mascagni's *Cavalleria rusticana* before writing *Jenůfa*, which received its premiere in Brno in 1904 (the same year as *Madama Butterfly*). The opera's grisly plot almost makes the verismo double-bill of "Cav-Pag" look tame. Set in a remote Moravian village in the late nineteenth century, it includes infanticide (by drowning) and a violent scene during which a jealous admirer slashes the face of his beloved. But the raw, verismo elements are balanced with Wagnerian themes of redemption and forgiveness.

Janáček uses the orchestra to convey both mood and setting, beginning with the repeated note on the xylophone that opens the opera, vividly evoking the clattering of the village watermill. Jenůfa (the stepdaughter of the Kostelnička, the stern chaplain and moral guardian of the village) is infatuated with her good-looking and wealthy drunkard cousin Števa, who has inherited the watermill, a valuable source of income. She is elated to learn that Števa, who has impregnated her, has not been conscripted and hopes he will marry her. The repeated xylophone note is heard again in the final scene in Act I, its ominous insistence a harbinger of the violence to unfold. Laca (Števa's half-brother), who is a laborer at the watermill and jealous of Števa's fortune, is in love with Jenůfa and tries to warn her of Števa's fickleness. "All he sees in you / are those rosy apple cheeks of yours," asserts Laca, the xylophone notes heard with increasing urgency as he sinisterly declares that "this knife might spoil them for you." The strings and winds play five-note motifs that swoop upward in anxious outbursts as Laca slashes Jenůfa's face, and then begs her forgiveness.

In Act II, Jenůfa gives birth, and the Kostelnička frets about the shame she has brought on the family. The Kostelnička's curt vocal lines and abrupt orchestral interjections contrast with music of radiant tenderness as Jenůfa soothes the baby. In a powerful and turbulent aria, the Kostelnička debates her options. She fights her conscience, the violins framing her words as she convinces herself that killing the baby is justified in order to save Jenůfa. Crime, guilt, punishment, forgiveness, and redemption come to the fore in Act III, when the villagers are stunned to discover that their moral guardian is a murderess. But Jenůfa understands the Kostelnička's motives and urges the villagers to give her a chance to repent. The Kostelnička then asks for Jenůfa's forgiveness, accompanied by music of rapturous beauty. In the ethereal conclusion, Jenůfa forgives Laca for cutting her face, singing, "You sinned only out of love, / just as I did—once upon a time." And when she gives him a chance to opt out of a marriage with a "disgraced" woman such as herself, he declares that her past doesn't matter.

Unlike Jenůfa, Tatiana Larina, the dreamy heroine of Tchaikovsky's *Eugene Onegin*, is unwilling and unable to take back the man who hurt her. With its aristocrats and palaces this is not a verismo opera, although the evolving relationship between the two main characters is certainly realistic and believable. Slavic opera blossomed in the nineteenth century, and *Eugene Onegin* is one of the most popular Russian operas. Tchaikovsky also wrote ballets, including *Swan Lake* and *The Nutcracker*, the *1812 Overture*, which is often played at July 4 celebrations in America, many symphonies, and other operas, including *The Queen of Spades*. Born in 1840 in Votkinsk, Russia, Tchaikovsky based *Eugene Onegin* (written in 1879) on Alexander Pushkin's hugely popular verse novel of the same name, focusing on the character Tatiana and her love affair with the dashing aristocrat Eugene Onegin. He patronizingly rebuffs the smitten young Tatiana when she sends him a love letter, telling her to get a grip on her emotions. That was perhaps something that Tchaikovsky could empathize with, since his music has been criticized for being overly emotional. Like Puccini's music, Tchaikovsky's is certainly heart-on-sleeve romantic and emotive, but what's wrong with that?

Tchaikovsky was an insecure man. He was tormented by the frequently harsh critiques of his music as well as by his homosexuality, which led him to abandon a brief and disastrous marriage. He died of cholera in 1893 after drinking contaminated water. He was supported throughout his career by a wealthy patron named Nadezhda von

Meck, whom he never met, but they corresponded regularly. When a singer colleague suggested that he turn Pushkin's famous work into a novel, Tchaikovsky initially resisted, feeling that the plot was insubstantial. But his music helped bring to the fore both the relationship between Tatiana and Onegin and her transformation from a naïve and insecure girl into a mature woman who controls her own destiny—although it turns out to be an unhappy one.

One of the most important scenes in the opera is Tatiana's extended "Letter Scene" in Act I. The music is lushly romantic as the girlish Tatiana dreams of love. She wonders if something is wrong with her and tears up the first draft of her letter to Onegin, the orchestra tenderly echoing her anxiety. She feels powerless to control her destiny and rues the day Onegin visited her family's countryside estate, sending her into turmoil. She recalls the effect his gaze had upon her and ponders whether he is her guardian angel or a dangerous tempter, her melodious questions framed by the winds and strings. Tatiana ends up marrying a prince, though, and by Act III there's little trace of the dreamy girl we first met. Onegin is amazed that the humble country girl he rejected has become such an alluring, confident woman, and he's immediately smitten when they meet again. But despite his rapturous pleas, Tatiana will not renounce her husband, even though she still loves Onegin. The opera concludes with a tender, remorseful duet as they lament their situation and Onegin rues his pitiful fate.

The velvety-voiced Russian soprano Anna Netrebko has offered a riveting portrayal of Tatiana in recent years, portraying with remarkable nuance Tatiana's evolution from innocent country girl to worldly sophisticate.

Netrebko's performance on the Live in HD production serves as a master class in character development. In the Letter Scene, Netrebko conveys Tatiana's flush of girlish excitement, her voice radiant and full, before singing in a hushed voice that she doesn't know how to begin her letter to Onegin. In this performance, we empathize with Tatiana's vulnerability and hope. At the end of the opera, Netrebko vividly illustrates not only the passion Tatiana still feels for Onegin, but also the character's strength and maturity as she resolutely declares she will not leave her husband. It's a remarkable performance by a gifted singing actress.

Pushkin also inspired other Russian operas, including Modest Mussorgsky's *Boris Godunov*, which tells the story of the czar who ruled Russia from 1598 to 1605 and—by legend, at least—instigated the murder of the young son of Ivan the Terrible, an heir to the throne. After some years of peace and prosperity, there is hunger and hardship, which some see as divine retribution for Boris's crime. With its elements of folk and liturgical music, this opera sounds more "Russian" than *Eugene Onegin*. Mussorgsky wrote gorgeous choral music for the majestic Coronation Scene, during which high and low brass notes alternate with relentless intensity, interwoven with a sinister beat gone haywire and a cacophony of bells, which indicate that an ominous cloud hangs over this coronation. The menacing atmosphere dissipates for a brief moment as the assembled crowd sings an ode to the glory of Russia and their new czar.

Bass voices have an important role in Russian choral and Orthodox church music, which sometimes features *oktavists*, basses who sing about an octave below the typical baritone range. This is the Queen of the Night effect in reverse: just as it's hard to imagine that a human voice can sing so high, it's also thrilling to hear a bass voice descend into what seems like an inhuman, gravelly low. Russian opera composers used the bass voice to evocative effect, as Mussorgsky did with the title role of Boris Godunov. In his gloomy monologue in the Coronation Scene, the reluctant czar sings of the dark premonitions he feels: "My soul is sad! A secret terror haunts me; / with evil presentiments my heart is stifled." When the Bulgarian bass Nicolai Ghiaurov, who died in 2004, performed the role, the rich, luxuriant sound of his voice imbued the words with a weighty gravitas. It would have been a very different effect if Mussorgsky had written this role for a tenor.

Critics often complain about the violence endemic to television and cinema, but the bloodshed on the opera stage is not for the faint of heart either. The stories of the works discussed in this chapter—in particular the blood and gore of Italian verismo—are hard hitting enough. But at the dawn of the twentieth century audiences were exposed to new operas of an even more brutal intensity, works that were shocking not just for the violent acts committed but for the depths of human insanity depicted. Strauss's character Salome, for example, makes Donizetti's Lucia seem only mildly deranged. Whereas the violent acts of the operas discussed so far are often accompanied by music that is lushly beautiful, the next generation of deranged protagonists were depicted with a musical language that seems an apt soundtrack to Edvard Munch's painting *The Scream*.

CHAPTER 5

FIN DE SIÈCLE DISSONANCE TO MIDCENTURY MELODY

ON STRAUSS, BERG, SHOSTAKOVICH, GERSHWIN, BRITTEN, AND OPERA IN TRANSLATION

BY THE TURN OF THE TWENTIETH CENTURY, OPERA-GOERS had been shocked by Wagner's R-rated sonic illustrations and by stories of lascivious gypsies, consumptive prostitutes, infanticide, and knife-wielding villagers. And then, in 1905, the German composer Richard Strauss outdid everyone with his psychodrama *Salome*, an X-rated opera that concludes with the heroine indulging in necrophilia. The first audience was thrilled: there were dozens of curtain calls at the premiere in Dresden in December 1905. But while *Salome* made Strauss a rich man, listeners weren't unanimous in their approval. After hearing a performance in Graz in 1906, Puccini wrote in a letter to a former pupil that he found the dissonant music "terribly cacophonous": he noted the "brilliant musical effects" but concluded that "in the end it's very tiring." The censors disapproved of the lurid story, and the ninety-minute opera was banned in some cities in Europe. In the British publication *Musical News*, an editorial declared that "the whole conception of the story is repugnant to Anglo-Saxon minds," adding, "it goes, in our opinion, beyond the limits of what is fit to be presented on the stage." After the opera received a single outing at the Metropolitan Opera in 1907, the Met's board (which included the financier J. P. Morgan, whose daughter was disturbed by the opera) canceled further performances. *Salome* wasn't heard at the Met again until 1934.

The world premiere in Paris of an introverted, fairy-tale opera called *Pelléas et Mélisande*, by the hugely influential French composer Claude Debussy in 1902, also attracted mixed reviews. One critic disparaged the "impressionism" of the work; another thought the voluptuous and sensual music "sickly" and "lifeless." In France, painters such as Monet and Renoir were focusing on mood and ambience, and Symbolist writers such as Charles Baudelaire, Paul Verlaine, and Maurice Maeterlinck were exploring spirituality, the imagination, and inner worlds. Maeterlinck's Symbolist play *Pelléas et Mélisande* inspired Debussy, who said "the drama of *Pelléas* which, despite its dream-like atmosphere, contains far more humanity than those so-called 'real-life documents.'...In it there is an evocative language whose sensitivity could be extended into music and into the orchestral decor." There are no arias in Debussy's *Pelléas*, which moves at a Wagnerian pace and whose mysterious, dreamy heroine is a polar opposite to a character like Tosca or Salome.

At the turn of the century in Germany, painters depicted emotions like grief and angst in a style known as *expressionism*, which emphasized negative feelings. Instead of trying to convey a realistic likeness when creating a portrait, for example, an expressionist artist focused instead on the subject's psychological state and tried to provoke an emotional reaction in the viewer. *Salome*, and another Strauss opera, *Elektra*, are often described as expressionist operas because the dissonant music depicts insanity to chilling effect and can leave the listener feeling shell-shocked. Strauss, born in 1864 to a well-off musical family in Munich, wrote many symphonic or "tone" poems, marvelous orchestral pieces that depict subjects from literature and visual art. *Salome*, a one-act opera scored for a huge orchestra, highlights the fin de siècle craze among artists for depicting sexually depraved women. It is based on Oscar Wilde's play *Salomé*, which was inspired in turn by the biblical story of Salome, Princess of Judea, who requested the head of John the Baptist when her stepfather, King Herod, delighted with her dancing, offered her a reward. After being presented with the head (on a platter), Salome gave it to her mother, Herodias, who was angry at the prophet because he had criticized her marriage to Herod Antipas as incestuous (she was his niece). Wilde spiced up this grisly story with an erotic element: Salome lusts after John, and Herod has the hots for Salome. Wilde believed that Salome's lust should be untamed "and her perversity without limits"—elements given full force in Strauss's opera, which is set in Galilee in the first century AD.

Strauss used dissonance to illustrate the title heroine's deranged state of mind. It is music of depraved sensuality and at times breathtakingly beautiful—a reminder that this is a love story, although certainly an obsessive and creepy one. In Puccini's *La bohème*, the music sounds entirely innocent: perhaps the antiestablishment bohemians are doing naughty things to keep warm in the garret, but a tender, G-rated soundtrack accompanies their moonlit declarations of love. The way Strauss depicts the moment of moonlit passion at the end of *Salome* is rather different.

The opera begins on the terrace of a banquet hall at King Herod's palace, where onlookers are admiring Salome's beauty. The sinewy clarinet line that slithers upward is an unsettling motif associated with her throughout the opera. Salome is intrigued by the sound of Jochanaan's (John the Baptist's) voice coming from the dungeon, announcing the coming of the Messiah and cursing Salome's mother. When Jochanaan is brought into the room, Salome is both repulsed and fascinated by his unkempt look. In these scenes, Strauss's music highlights both the prophet's religious devotion and Salome's increasing attraction to him. Jochanaan's sonorous rejections only excite her more. She is accompanied by harp ripples as she compares his voice to celestial music. Salome praises his ivory skin and asks to touch him, but Jochanaan refuses. She then calls him a leper and claims his "body is hideous," "like a plastered wall, where vipers have crawled" and "scorpions have made their nest." The music is eerily seductive as he again rebuffs her; accompanied by sinister-sounding music, she describes his hair as "horrible." Finally, she confesses that she wants to kiss him, repeating her plea multiple times as Jochanaan curses her and urges her to seek redemption. The frenzied music echoes Salome's derangement, and the scene concludes with a wild orchestral postlude in which the strings soar over riotous percussion. A growly line played by bassoon indicates that the prophet has gone back down to his cistern, the notes fading away against a relentless, agitated tremolo in the strings. Then it's Salome's turn to do the rejecting: after rebuffing her lecherous stepfather, she agrees to dance for him, but only after he promises whatever she demands as a reward.

For the title role, Strauss had hoped to find "a 16-year-old princess with the voice of an Isolde." Instead, the theater cast the Dresden soprano Marie Wittich, who had the voice of an Isolde but not the figure of a teenager. She protested that she could not possibly enact what she called the "perversities" of the lascivious "Dance of the Seven Veils," in which Salome strips until nude for Herod. (During the premiere, a body double did the dance: some singers are now willing to adhere to the original stage directions.) Against the wishes of her mother, Salome does a slow, sultry dance for her stepfather. Woodwinds play sinewy, "exotic"-sounding melodies against flickers of percussion. "Wonderful, wonderful," cries Herod after watching her dance. In an understated voice that belies the gruesome request she is making, Salome demands Jochanaan's head on a platter, and a horrified outburst from the brass instruments follows. In a panic, Herod tries to convince her to accept jewels, peacocks, even land instead, but his fearful outbursts meet only with Salome's rebuttals. She demands the head of Jochanaan after each of his pleas, her words at first imbued with a sinister calm that becomes increasingly savage.

The orchestra illustrates this disturbing scene with cacophonous swirls of sound that conclude with an abrupt silence. The executioner descends to the cistern, and when he brings forth the head of Jochanaan on a platter, and Salome seizes it, the orchestra explodes in what sounds like a shriek. During her ensuing monologue Salome addresses the prophet's head, asking why he never let her kiss him. The music in this horrific scene is wild, beautiful, and even tender at times—a deranged *Liebestod* ("love-death," a literary term meaning the consummation of love in or after death) that builds toward the satisfaction of Salome's erotic longing. "She is monstrous," Herod—trembling with fear—tells Herodias over an ominous drumbeat. A long trill sounds a harbinger of doom before Salome sings, softly, that she has finally kissed Jochanaan. The trill continues to unfold, a relentless drone, as she declares that the taste of love is bitter. The orchestra then soars in ecstatic surges as a ray of moonlight illuminates Salome, and the musical radiance is shattered by a jarring, dissonant chord that seems to cement her downfall into depravity. Herod orders his soldiers to kill her.

Strauss dealt with extremes of mental instability and neurosis even more probingly in *Elektra*, which was based on the Greek tragedy by Sophocles about the demise of the House of Agamemnon. The Viennese poet Hugo von Hofmannsthal, who had written a play on the same subject and wrote the libretto, was familiar with Sigmund Freud's writings about women, sexuality, and mental instability. In the ninety-minute, one-act opera, set a few years after the end of the Trojan War, Elektra obsesses about the murder of her father (Agamemnon) by her mother, Klytämnestra (Clytemnestra), and her mother's lover, Aegisth (Aegisthus), and plots revenge. Elektra hopes to enlist her brother Orest (Orestes, whom she hasn't seen in years) and her gentle sister, Chrysothemis (a neurotic who wants no part of Elektra's crazed plans for revenge), to help her.

Strauss used a huge orchestra for the opera, which opens with three notes (a leitmotif for Agamemnon) that culminate in a dramatic chord. The music is even wilder and more dissonant than that of *Salome*; it reportedly displeased King George V, who was disturbed by the cacophony when he heard a royal band play some of the music in the courtyard of Buckingham Palace. As in *Salome*, in *Elektra* Strauss used dissonance to convey the inner workings of a deranged mind; the harshness of some of the music contrasts with a sweeping lyricism that highlights moments of tenderness and accompanies the milder characters like Chrysothemis. In one chilling scene, the guilt-ridden, insomniac Klytämnestra tells Elektra about her recurring nightmares:

> *When I, with eyes wide open, sleepless lie,*
> *a Something creeps o'er my couch.*
> *It is no word, it is no pain,*
> *it hath no weight, it chokes me not…*
> *But in truth it doth so madden me,*
> *the hangman's rope would less appall my soul.*

The brass instruments accompany Klytämnestra's ghoulish depictions with swooping, slithering motifs. When the distraught Klytämnestra ponders the idea of a sacrifice to the gods to alleviate her suffering, she is horrified to hear Elektra inform her that she—Klytämnestra—will be the human sacrifice. Orest murders Klytämnestra and Aegisth, and the opera concludes with an eerily turbulent waltz as Elektra dances herself to death.

The lushly romantic music and sumptuous love duets of *Der Rosenkavalier* (*The Knight of the Rose*)—which premiered in 1911, two years after *Elektra*—sound like the work of a different composer. *Rosenkavalier*, a comic opera set in Vienna in the mid-eighteenth century, with a libretto by Von Hofmannsthal, tells the story of the aristocratic Marschallin, a thirty-two-year-old married woman who considers herself already "of a certain age." (A *Marschallin* is the wife of a field marshal.) She certainly has her troubles, but her dignity (and sanity) are all the more striking compared to the deranged Elektra and Salome. The Marschallin is having an affair with the teenage Octavian (a trouser role), and pathos and comedy are interwoven as they are in Mozart's *Marriage of Figaro* (which influenced *Rosenkavalier*). But whereas Mozart's Countess is nostalgic for past joys, the Marschallin fears that her current happiness will soon elude her. She is mourning the passing of time and worries that Octavian will abandon her for a younger woman. This comes to pass when Octavian is asked to present an engagement rose to the beautiful young Sophie from a suitor, and the two instantly become smitten with each other. The opera concludes with a ravishing trio for the Marschallin, Sophie, and Octavian. In his will,

Strauss asked that this trio be sung at his funeral (which took place in Munich in 1949, upon his death at the age of eighty-five).

In the scenes leading up to the trio, Octavian has been busy with a farcical ploy to help Sophie avoid a miserable marriage to her boorish older suitor, Baron Ochs. As in the *Marriage of Figaro*, after all the confusion, cross-dressing comedy, and general hubbub, the characters are suitably paired off—and all the wiser and more emotionally mature after their experiences. In the trio, the Marschallin admits that she promised to cede Octavian to a younger woman, but is sad that it has all transpired so quickly. She sings a heartbreakingly beautiful, introspective melody before Sophie (who is overwhelmed by the situation) and Octavian (who is conflicted between his two loves) join in. After expressing their initial doubts, the three characters are of the same mind: Sophie and Octavian declare their love, and the Marschallin gives them her blessing, the three voices soaring in rapturous synergy. It's utterly gorgeous.

STRAUSS'S ATTACK ON THE TONAL STATUS QUO IN *ELEKTRA* followed centuries of experimentation. Opera composers had been crossing the harmonic threshold since the seventeenth century, when Monteverdi used startling dissonances to heighten the expressive impact of the text. In the nineteenth and early twentieth centuries, composers such as Wagner and Debussy both pushed tonality out of its comfort zone. But it was Arnold Schoenberg and his pupil Alban Berg who caused a seismic shift with music that is *atonal*, meaning it lacks a key or tonal center. In atonal music, dissonances are not expected to resolve into consonance, and composers use the twelve notes of the chromatic scale instead of only the seven notes of the major and minor scales. Because tonal centers and the hierarchical relationships inherent in major and minor scales are not present in atonal music, each of these twelve notes can be equally important in an atonal work. Schoenberg, who called for the "emancipation of the dissonance," wanted to liberate music from what he saw as the orthodoxy of the conventional tonal system. Atonal music uses a completely different palette of sounds from that of *Carmen*, *Tosca*, and other primarily tonal operas. Audience members certainly do not come away from Alban Berg's *Wozzeck* humming any tunes. But since Berg wasn't dogmatic about sticking to rules, and didn't reject tonality entirely, the music retains a romantic expressivity.

Berg, an Austrian composer born in 1885 to a wealthy Viennese family, was entranced when in 1914 he saw the play *Woyzeck* by Georg Büchner, based on a true story about a working-class soldier who in 1821 murdered his mistress. Before committing this crime, the title character of the play becomes the victim of physical and psychological abuse when he is subjected to sadistic experiments by the army doctor—as well as the tyranny of his demanding captain. Berg, who had a stint in an army training camp, empathized with such downtrodden characters, writing to his wife that he himself had spent the war years "dependent on people I hate, in chains, sick, captive, resigned, in fact, humiliated." *Wozzeck*, Berg's ninety-minute opera, explores issues of social alienation, power, and poverty and how these factors can propel an ordinary (and fundamentally good) man to murder someone he loves. The sadistic doctor who accelerates his breakdown represents a hostile society; Marie, Wozzeck's common-law wife and the mother of his child, is independent and unfaithful, although she is also a doting mother. (Berg himself had fathered an illegitimate child with a household maid named Marie.) The premiere of this expressionist and mostly atonal opera at the Berlin State Opera in 1925 was a success, and the theater scheduled additional performances, but some critics hated it: one compared leaving the opera house after the performance to exiting an insane asylum and described the opera as a "capital offense."

Berg created a remarkable sound world to convey different moods and settings. One of these is in the twilight forest scene of Act III, when Marie and Wozzeck stroll together and he makes cryptic comments about fidelity. Here the orchestral music is eerily subdued, the quietly agitated mutterings in the woodwinds sounding a warning. "How red the moon rises!" sings Marie—her notes ascending with slow insistence. Wozzeck responds, "Like a bloody blade," as a steady drumbeat increases the tension. Wozzeck then stabs Marie with a knife. "Dead!" he declares. After an eerie calm the orchestra plays a crescendo on a single note, which culminates in a jarring chord. The crescendo is repeated, accompanied by a drum roll, and increases in intensity until suddenly morphing—with a brilliant and disorienting flash—into the honky-tonk piano polka of the ensuing bar scene.

In the penultimate scene, Wozzeck returns to the forest to retrieve the knife, but becomes increasingly disoriented. As Strauss did to highlight Elektra's insanity, Berg uses dissonance to psychologically potent effect in a brutal musical depiction of Wozzeck's mental breakdown. "Murder! Murder! They'll be looking for me....The knife will betray me!" Wozzeck declares. "I wash myself in blood! The water is blood...blood...," are his last words as he wades into the pond. The agitated rising scales in the wind and string instruments create a suffocating effect as the water rises above him and he drowns. Berg used an expressionist vocal technique called *Sprechgesang*, which (like recitative) blends elements of speech and singing. The style might sound strange upon first hearing to a newcomer to opera, but it can be used to vivid theatrical effect. This is the case in the uneven vocal lines vividly evoking Wozzeck's disturbed frame of mind. His hallucinatory declarations sound truly spooky: it's not supposed to be a comfortable experience for the listener.

Berg died in 1935 of blood poisoning caused by an insect bite before completing the orchestration for his opera *Lulu*, whose titular heroine is the ultimate femme fatale. (The opera premiered in Zurich in 1937 in a two-act version; Act III was orchestrated by the composer Friedrich Cerha in the 1970s, and the complete opera was first performed in 1979.) Berg was inspired to write *Lulu* after seeing two plays by the German playwright Frank Wedekind, who critiqued the hypocrisy of a bourgeois society in which men frequented brothels but denounced prostitutes as debauched. Lulu is a heartless, manipulative, amoral character who dominates her victims physically and emotionally; she is blithely unconcerned when the Physician (her husband) drops dead after discovering one of her affairs. She then marries the Painter, who kills himself after learning about her sexual past; after that, she disrupts the wealthy Dr. Schön's engagement to another woman and marries him herself. She retains a phalanx of admirers, including a lesbian countess, an acrobat, a schoolboy, and Dr. Schön's son, Alwa. After Lulu kills Dr. Schön, she is arrested; later she becomes a prostitute. One of her customers is Jack the Ripper, who murders her as well as the adoring countess. Berg stipulated that the singers portraying Lulu's husbands should also sing the role of her clients in the same performance. Berg used Schoenberg's twelve-tone technique—in which all twelve notes of the chromatic scale are equally important, and notes are arranged in sequences called *tone rows.*

The Nazis banned both *Wozzeck* and *Lulu* and labeled them "degenerate"—a term they applied to modern art and music they deemed Jewish, communist, or simply un-German. The fascists wanted classical music and opera to be populist, easy to digest, and free of foreign influences, such as jazz.

The authorities also censored music extensively in the Soviet Union, including both operas written by Dmitri Shostakovich, who was born in 1906 in St. Petersburg. As a twenty-year-old student, he had been in the audience for the 1927 Leningrad premiere of *Wozzeck.* Shostakovich's first opera, inspired by Nikolai Gogol's satirical story "The Nose," had been criticized for its avant-garde elements, but it was with *Lady Macbeth of the Mtsensk District,* his next opera, that Shostakovich received his first truly ominous warning. Composers whose music was deemed too avant-garde were denounced as "formalist" and pressured to adhere to the socialist realism aesthetic and create works that could be used as propaganda tools. The music was supposed to be accessible to a wide audience, cheery in nature, and capable of inspiring patriotic devotion. *Lady Macbeth of the Mtsensk District* certainly proved accessible: it was a hit at its premiere in 1934 in Leningrad, and widely performed over the next two years in Russia; it was also heard in Europe and in North and South America. But when Stalin walked out of a new production in 1936 at the Bolshoi in Moscow, the opera was denounced soon afterward. An anonymous editorial called "Muddle Instead of Music" appeared in *Pravda,* the official Communist Party newspaper. From the very start of the opera, it said, "listeners are stunned by the deliberately dissonant and confused stream of sounds...singing is replaced by screaming...the music quacks, hoots, pants and gasps in order to express the love scenes as naturally as possible." If Shostakovich kept this up, warned the editorial, things might not end well. After this attack, Shostakovich never finished another opera. Many of his ensuing string quartets and symphonies sound like the internal soundtrack of a composer constantly on the verge of a panic attack: the music glistens with a paranoid edge that hints of scurrying footsteps and fierce knocks at the door.

The *Pravda* article implies that *Lady Macbeth* is a challenging, cacophonous few hours in the theater, but with its traditional, sometimes even tuneful vocal writing, rhythmic propulsion, folkish choruses, and vaudeville references, the music is not "difficult"—the opera is more "accessible" than *Lulu* or *The Nose*. But the story, which includes brutal murders and a sex scene, all graphically depicted in the music, didn't exactly fit the Soviet bill for wholesome family entertainment. Shostakovich described *Lady Macbeth* as "tragedy-satire." It's based on a story by Nikolai Leskov about a lonely housewife (Katerina Izmailova) who is trapped in a loveless marriage and bullied by her lecherous father-in-law, Boris. She has an affair with a handsome, brutish laborer, Sergei, and together they murder her husband, the wealthy merchant Zinovy, whose corpse is discovered on the day of their nuptials, leading to their arrest. En route to prison camp in Siberia, Sergei leaves Katerina for a fellow convict, Sonyetka; Katerina then drowns herself and her rival.

The opera features music of both funereal beauty and circus-like debauchery. In the opening scene Katerina sings of her depression and boredom, her lyrical, haunting vocal lines elegantly accompanied by strings and winds. Shostakovich rendered the operatic Katerina as a much more sympathetic character than she was in her literary incarnation in Gogol's story. She sings again of her misery and thwarted desires later in Act I, in a plaintively beautiful, passionate aria called "The foal runs after the filly." But when Katerina and Sergei consummate their affair, Shostakovich reveals his sardonic side, unafraid to mince notes in a brazen musical depiction replete with brash trombone glissandi and other unsubtle musical effects. The composer represents the other characters with grotesque, carnival-like music: Boris is introduced with a coarse, lurching bassoon melody, which indicates his bullying character. At the beginning of Act II, when Boris recalls how he used to seduce married women and makes a pass at Katerina, Shostakovich accompanies his actions with a distorted Viennese waltz. Shostakovich wants the audience to empathize with Katerina: she may be a murderess, but it's hard not to feel sorry for her when she reveals her sorrow in a moving lament accompanied by a solo English horn (a woodwind instrument that resembles an oboe but has a lower range).

IN ADDITION TO BEING FREQUENTLY CENSORED FOR ITS potential to offend royalty or other dignitaries, opera has often served as a vehicle to moralize, to flatter patrons, and even to disseminate political and cultural propaganda. During the Cold War, the US State Department used the opera *Porgy and Bess* by the American composer George Gershwin, which featured poor African Americans as protagonists, as a propaganda tool in the Soviet Union and elsewhere to showcase American artistic achievement. The casts for the touring productions were African American, and US officials tried to promote the notion that race relations had improved and opportunities for minorities were expanding. The Mississippi-born African American soprano Leontyne Price, one of the most important singers of the twentieth century, adored for her radiant and powerful voice, sang the role of Bess during a European tour of the opera in 1952. When Price (who turned ninety in 2017) sang the title role in Puccini's *Tosca* for a televised production on the American network NBC in 1955, however, some affiliates of the station in various American cities were unwilling to air the performance because of her race.

While the Soviet authorities disliked European modernism, they approved of Gershwin's tuneful and accessible style, perhaps an ironic affinity in light of Gershwin's use of popular American styles and the ostensible Soviet dislike of all things American. The opening number, "Summertime," became a popular jazz standard. It blends folk, blues, jazz, and possibly a Ukrainian lullaby, an eclecticism that reflects the composer's background and interests. Born in 1898 in Brooklyn, New York, to Russian Jewish immigrants, Gershwin played both classical and ragtime piano and wrote his own spirituals for *Porgy*, which incorporates jazz, blues, and gospel into a standard operatic template of arias and recitative. The opera—set in the 1920s in Catfish Row (an area of tenement housing in Charleston, South Carolina)—is based on a 1925 novel by Edwin DuBose Heyward about a love triangle between Porgy (a character inspired by news reports about a local panhandler accused of murder), Bess (a beautiful drug addict), and the murderous Crown. Heyward was a white southerner who had grown up in Charleston, and he was familiar with the local Gullah culture among the blacks of the region. He was both praised and criticized for his novel. The African American poet Langston Hughes approved of his empathetic treatment of the residents of Catfish Row; others criticized the novel and opera (which has a libretto by Heyward along with Ira Gershwin, George's brother) for perpetuating stereotypes of drugs, crime, and poverty in the black community. The opera fell out of favor in the civil rights era, and some black artists became reluctant to perform in it, or even refused.

There are many memorable arias in the opera in addition to "Summertime," such as the toe-tapping "A Woman Is a Sometime Thing," Porgy's "I Got Plenty o' Nuttin'," and the drug dealer Sportin' Life's "It Ain't Necessarily So"—which is interwoven with gospel-tinged choral music. A passionate duet between Porgy and Bess ("Bess, You Is My Woman") is Puccini-like in its soaring lyricism, as is Bess's aria "I Loves You, Porgy." The opera concludes with a gospel-inspired number called "O Lawd, I'm on My Way." Since the turn of the millennium it has been staged as both musical theater and opera, and despite the many controversies it has sparked, *Porgy* is now widely appreciated as a masterpiece.

Gershwin had been offered a commission from the Metropolitan Opera to write a grand opera in an American idiom, but he wanted *Porgy* to be performed by black singers, not by white actors in blackface. This was impossible during that era—no black singers were then allowed to perform at the Met. (In 1955, the contralto Marian Anderson became the first African American artist to sing there.) So *Porgy* was instead booked for a run on Broadway in 1935 with a cast of classically trained black singers. It received mixed reviews and was not commercially successful. Revivals on Broadway featured a shortened musical-theater version, with a pared-down orchestra and recitatives replaced by spoken dialogue. In 1985, thirty years after it played at La Scala, *Porgy* was finally presented (in its original version) at the Metropolitan Opera. At the request of the Gershwin estate, black singers are always hired to sing the leading roles in the United States. Productions in Europe featuring white casts, including one at the Hungarian State Opera in 2018, have been controversial. The Gershwin estate asked the Hungarian company to specify in printed materials that the staging was "contrary to the requirements for the presentation of the work."

Gershwin wrote an article, published in the *New York Times* in 1935, about the origins of *Porgy*. He explained why he considered it a folk opera: "When I first began work on the music I decided against the use of original folk material because I wanted the music to be all of one piece. Therefore I wrote my own spirituals and folksongs. But they are still folk music—and therefore, being in operatic form, 'Porgy and Bess' becomes a folk opera." Gershwin, who died in 1937 at thirty-eight from a brain tumor, explained that he had wanted to create "something in American music that would appeal to the many rather than to the cultured few." He chose opera because he believed that "music lives only when it is in serious form."

The German Jewish composer Kurt Weill also used art to explore the social issues of his era and to advocate for change. Weill, an émigré composer who fled Nazi Germany in 1933 and moved to America in 1935, was another master of blending idioms like jazz and folk into classical templates. Weill wanted to break free of operatic convention and strove to create what he called "a special brand of musical theater which would completely integrate drama and music, spoken word, song and movement." He is best known for his *Threepenny Opera*—a critique of capitalism done in collaboration with the playwright Bertolt Brecht that premiered in Berlin in 1928. Adapted from John Gay's *Beggar's Opera*, its best-known excerpt is "Mack the Knife," a song about a murderer in which satirical, mocking words are set to jaunty music. Just as Gershwin's "Summertime" spawned myriad covers, "The Alabama Song" from Weill's satirical opera *Rise and Fall of the City of Mahagonny* inspired The Doors' "Alabama Song (Whisky Bar)," as well as a cover by David Bowie. Weill's opera *Street Scene*, based on a 1929 play by Elmer Rice, and with a libretto by Langston Hughes, tells the story of a diverse group of residents in a tenement block on a scorching summer day in 1940s New York, the ideal setting for Weill's melting-pot aesthetic of jazz, blues, and Puccini-like arias. Weill referred to *Street Scene*, first performed on Broadway in 1947, as "American opera" and "Broadway opera."

Ten years after the premiere of *Porgy and Bess*, Benjamin Britten's *Peter Grimes*—a hit at its premiere in London in 1945—was heralded as the first great English opera since Purcell's *Dido and Aeneas*. (There were a handful of operas by English and Irish composers that were popular in Britain in the late nineteenth century but seldom performed after World War I.) Britten was influenced by *Porgy and Bess* and, like Gershwin, wanted his music to be accessible to a wide public. Britten was born in 1913 in the English fishing village of Lowestoft to a dentist father and a singer mother who had lofty ambitions for her musically precocious son. She declared that he would become the fourth "B"—following in the footsteps of Bach, Beethoven, and Brahms. Many opera composers throughout the centuries had focused on works for the theater, and often their rare forays into other genres, such as Verdi's String Quartet, are unmemorable. But Britten, like Mozart, flourished in myriad genres: in addition to his successful operas, Britten wrote symphonies, string quartets, concertos, and pieces for solo instruments. The festival he founded in 1948 in Aldeburgh, near his birthplace on the east coast of England, is still going strong.

Britten's operas feature a theme close to his heart—that of the outsider rejected by the community. A pacifist and conscientious objector during World War II, he lived openly as a gay man at a time when homosexuality was illegal; he composed many of the central roles in his operas for his life partner, the great tenor Peter Pears. Britten was questioned by Scotland Yard during the 1950s, when several prominent men suspected of being gay were put on trial in England. The American conductor Leonard Bernstein once said that Britten's music may seem "decorative, positive and charming," but added that "it's so much more than that.... You become aware of something very dark....He was a man at odds with the world in many ways." But Britten was also part of the British establishment, a respected figure who was commissioned to write music for important state events. (When he died at the age of sixty-three, Queen Elizabeth II sent Pears a letter of condolence.) Britten's operas include *Death in Venice*, based on the Thomas Mann novella about an older man's obsession with a beautiful adolescent, and the chamber work *The Turn of the Screw*, based on the Henry James ghost story about two children haunted by the ghosts of former servants. (The corruption of innocence is another theme prevalent in Britten's works.) In his opera *Billy Budd* (which has an all-male cast and is based on the Melville novel), Britten depicted the clash between good and evil as personified by two sailors.

Britten, who wanted listeners to enjoy his works, was scorned by some of his avant-garde colleagues, who often alienated audiences with their own impenetrable, academic music. But while Britten derided the music of Schoenberg and other modernist composers, he didn't reject their new techniques entirely: the gorgeous music of *The Turn of the Screw* incorporates twelve-tone technique within a melodic, tonal framework. His scores also reflect many other influences, including English folk traditions and Indonesian gamelan music (a genre using an ensemble of instruments including gongs, bamboo flutes, and xylophones).

Britten evoked the rugged, bleak countryside of his childhood to stunning effect in *Peter Grimes*, which was inspired by a narrative poem by the eighteenth-century British writer George Crabbe about a fisherman outcast whose two young apprentices die. The unequivocally evil Grimes of Crabbe's poem is a more ambiguous character in the opera—a rough-tempered outcast, certainly, but also the victim of a mean, judgmental, hypocritical society. Britten said the subject matter was close to his heart—describing it as "the struggle of the individual against the masses." "The more vicious the society, the more vicious the individual," he said. Set to text by the communist writer Montagu Slater, the vocal lines adhere to the natural inflections and rhythms of the English language, both when set to music and in a cappella format.

Composers such as Rossini and Wagner depicted natural events and panoramas, such as the alpine vistas of *Guillaume Tell* and the violent storm of *Die Walküre*, with the precision of fine landscape painters. In *Peter Grimes*, the sea becomes almost like another character. Britten conveys its moods so vividly that you feel transported to the gray, windswept beaches of an isolated fishing village. Four of the six remarkable orchestral interludes that are woven through the opera were published separately as the "Sea Interludes" and are frequently performed in symphonic concerts. In "On the Beach," the first orchestral interlude, violins play in unison in a high register, their somber line punctuated by swooping, whirling arpeggios. The ominous declarations of the brass instruments hint at a violent, threatening sea. "The Storm," the second interlude, is a brilliant depiction of a tempest: the music seethes and swells in dramatic crests before receding into an occasional moment of calm. In "Sunday Morning by the Beach," which is punctuated by church bells, the music is cheerier but still restless. The cries of seagulls are vividly evoked by wind instruments. In the fourth interlude, a cello plays a forlorn tune over the stately pizzicatos of the double basses. The increasing urgency of the music alludes to the impending disaster.

The chorus, whose gorgeous music often incorporates English folk songs and hymns, represents the villagers of the Borough, who are suspicious of Grimes and think he's guilty even after the death of the first apprentice at sea has been ruled accidental. Grimes has few allies, except for the kind schoolteacher Ellen Orford, whom he wants to marry. Grimes is told he must hire a grown man as his next assistant, but he defiantly takes on a local boy named John instead. As a mob of townspeople approach his hut, Grimes tells John to clamber down the cliff and quickly board the fishing boat, and the boy slips and falls to his death. Grimes once again comes under suspicion when Ellen finds a sweater she made for the boy washed up on the beach.

In Britten's opera, Grimes's guilt is a matter of interpretation. When Peter Pears originated the part in 1945, he portrayed Grimes as a sensitive, intelligent dreamer and the victim of mob mentality, a frail outsider with whom the audience could empathize. Pears's lyric tenor voice sounded very different, however, from the gruffer tone of Jon Vickers (discussed in the Wagner chapter), another notable interpreter of Grimes. Vickers, the son of a Baptist preacher, was said to be a homophobe. He had a notoriously volcanic personality and a habit of lashing out at fellow singers and conductors. Britten disapproved of his raw and violent interpretation, about which one critic wrote: "His voice is like a long plaint, a groan, the cry of a wild beast, a drunken chant of beauty and distress which soars above the maddened crowd."

At the end of the opera, the villagers embark on a manhunt to find Grimes:

Who holds himself apart,
Lets his pride rise
Him who despises us
We'll destroy

The voices of the chorus become clipped as they sing this section:

Our curse shall fall upon his evil day; We shall destroy.
We shall Tame his arrogance!
Ha, Ha, Ha, Ha…we'll make the murderer pay for
his crime.

The orchestral music adds an extra frisson of unease to these already chilling words. "Peter Grimes, Peter Grimes," the villagers cry out in seemingly endless repetition in the final, harrowing scenes. Grimes loses his mind and veers between quiet musings and aggrieved outbursts in an a cappella lament. After he moors his boat and hears the townsfolk calling his name from afar, he starts repeating his name himself, stretching his surname into tortured melismas. The chorus intones his name as he mournfully sings, "What harbor shelters peace, away from tidal waves, / away from storms!" At the urging of a local retired captain, Grimes takes the boat back out to sea and never returns. When Vickers sang the role at the Royal Opera House in 1981, during his final moments on stage he slowly bowed his head in a brief moment of what could be resignation, guilt, or despair—or perhaps, all three. Then he defiantly swaggered off to his boat.

At the end of the opera life in the village continues as usual: we hear the rippling arpeggios of the opening interlude once again as the chorus sings in unison: "In ceaseless motion comes and goes the tide..."

THE TIDE CERTAINLY TURNED FOR ENGLISH-LANGUAGE opera with *Peter Grimes*. Some of the most significant works of recent decades feature English librettos, and Italian, long a staple of opera, is not the lingua franca of twenty-first-century opera. The idiosyncrasies of a particular language are integral to opera, whether it's the colloquial English used in *Porgy and Bess* or the German text of *Salome*. The relative supremacy of words or music (and which comes first) is opera's version of the chicken-or-the-egg debate, which Strauss explored in *Capriccio* (1942), where a poet and a composer bicker about the question, each hoping to seduce a countess with his own art form. Salieri, a contemporary and rival of Mozart, had already parodied the aesthetic tussles (and histrionic divas) in a comic one-act opera called *Prima la musica, poi le parole* (*First the Music, Then the Words*). In this work, a poet struggles to produce a libretto on short notice for a finished score, and then resorts to recycling some of his old verses to fit the music. In most cases, however, a composer sets about composing the score after receiving the libretto.

Although music is certainly the dominant force in opera, the libretto is of course the fundamental building block, and thus the issue of language barriers has been prevalent

almost since the birth of opera. On one level, you can derive much pleasure from listening to the operatic voice
even without knowing what the artist is singing about:
the "Three Tenors"—Pavarotti, Domingo, and Carreras—
seduced legions of fans with their glorious voices even
though many listeners may not have been familiar with the
text or context of a particular aria. In a wonderful scene
in the film *The Shawshank Redemption*, directed by Frank
Darabont, the prisoner Andy Dufresne irks his captors by
blasting a recording of the duet "Sull'aria…che soave zeffiretto" (On the breeze…what a gentle little zephyr) from
Mozart's *Marriage of Figaro* through the prison sound system. Every man in the courtyard stops and listens, their
faces turned upward in rapt attention. "I have no idea to
this day what those two Italian ladies were singing about,"
says the prisoner played by the actor Morgan Freeman.
"Truth is, I don't want to know. Some things are best left
unsaid. I'd like to think they were singing about something
so beautiful, it can't be expressed in words, and it makes
your heart ache because of it. I tell you, those voices soared
higher and farther than anybody in a great place dares to
dream. It was like some beautiful bird flapped into our
drab little cage and made those walls dissolve away, and for
the briefest of moments, every last man at Shawshank felt
free." The two soprano voices intertwine with such seductive elegance in this duet that if you don't understand the
lyrics you might well assume the women are singing about
something delightful, but in fact, the Countess is dictating
a letter that will lure her husband into an illicit encounter
and prove his infidelity.

Sung text in opera—even in a familiar language, and even if the singer has impeccable diction—is invariably more difficult to decipher than spoken text. This is particularly true when a vowel is elongated and elaborately ornamented, three one-syllable words are stretched out with melismatic flourishes, or multiple voices join forces in a musically complex sextet. In many operas of the late Romantic and the early twentieth-century periods, a lone voice must often project over large and loud instrumental ensembles: a poetic David facing a musical Goliath. Text is invariably more difficult to understand when sung in a higher female range, and at its most stratospheric the words are usually unintelligible. In the earliest days of opera, listeners were often provided with a printed copy of the text, even when they understood the language in question. Audience members at the premiere of Monteverdi's *L'Orfeo* were given copies of the libretto to follow during the performance, for example, even though they spoke Italian, the language of the opera.

While watching a foreign film with no subtitles seems a pointless endeavor if you don't speak the language, operagoers can derive enormous pleasure from listening to opera even without knowing why the soprano is so distressed, or why the baritone is about to murder someone—just as the Shawshank prisoners are held spellbound by the Mozart duet they hear in Darabont's film. But if you want to understand the story and appreciate the way a singer delivers the text, then you do need to understand the words.

The opera world became more welcoming to new audiences with the introduction of Surtitles—the trademarked name for lyrics projected above the stage—in the 1980s. In January 1983, the Canadian Opera Company (which registered the trademark) projected translations on a screen above the stage during its production of *Elektra*, and the New York City Opera introduced similar "super-titles" later that year. The introduction of translations projected above the stage or on the seat in front of a viewer allowed a broader audience to enjoy opera, although some in the opera industry initially resisted the innovation: detractors claimed that supertitles would distract the audience and draw attention away from the performers. Surtitles can certainly be cumbersome if audience members have to swivel their heads to read them, but given the frequent (and sometimes confusing) plot twists in opera, the benefits of translations vastly outweigh any potential downsides.

That's assuming you have a colloquial adaptation, however. The translation for "Sull'aria...che soave zeffiretto," the aria heard in *The Shawshank Redemption*, might use the word "zephyr," but since "zephyr" is not commonly used in modern speech, that translation isn't particularly helpful. No one says, "A gentle zephyr will sigh this evening." Thus supertitles must use colloquial language—otherwise audiences will be listening to a language they possibly don't understand while reading supertitles that themselves almost need to be translated. There are other challenges when adapting text for sung versions as well. A translator of any literary work must honor the original writer's style and intended meaning, but opera linguists face the additional challenge of ensuring that the words adhere to the rhythms of the music. In "Non più andrai, farfallone amoroso" (You won't go anymore, amorous butterfly), the final aria of Act I in *The Marriage of Figaro*, the title character admonishes the flirtatious Cherubino that his amorous exploits will end in the army. The translation of the opening line is often rendered in a way that would sound cumbersome if sung (another version is "Amorous butterfly, you won't flit about day and night"). The Italian words neatly fit the bouncy rhythm of the music, while the literally translated English words do not. A translation by Jeremy Sams is snappy, effective, and fits the music:

> *Here's an end to your life as a rover*
> *Here's an end to the young Casanova.*
> *It was fun for a while, but it's over;*
> *We will soon wipe the smile off your face.*

Figaro's "Se vuol ballare" in Act I is sometimes translated as

> *If you would dance, my pretty Count*
> *I'll play the tune on my little guitar.*
> *If you will come to my dancing school*
> *I'll gladly teach you the capriole.*

But since most of us are unfamiliar with the "capriole," the subversive nature of the aria is lost in translation. Sams offers us a much clearer idea of the subtleties of the situation with the following translation:

So, little master, you're dressed to go dancing,
dressed in your best to go strutting and prancing.
I'll put an end to your fun pretty soon;
you may go dancing but I'll call the tune, yes,
I'll call the tune.

In 2011 the poet J. D. McClatchy published a book of verse translations of seven Mozart librettos to show English-language readers the literary merit of the original German and Italian texts. He also created a sung translation of Mozart's *Magic Flute*, used in the Metropolitan Opera's abridged family matinee and a fine example of a German libretto aptly translated into singable English. In the aria "Der Vogelfänger, bin ich ja" (I'm Papageno, that's my name), the words are compatible with the rhythms of the music:

I'm Papageno, that's my name.
And catching birds, well, that's my game!
My snares are laid. My sights are set.
I whistle them into my net.
My life's my own, so bright and free,
for all the birds belong to me.
If only there were traps for girls,
I'd catch a dozen by their curls.

Sometimes the aural impact of a particular word is invariably lost in translation. *Vendetta*, for example, a ubiquitous word in Italian opera, means "revenge" or "vengeance," and the sonorities of the Italian render the meaning more immediately ferocious. Ditto *ingrata* (ungrateful) and *maledizione* (curse).

In addition to translating text to singable English or using contemporary slang in supertitles, writers occasionally go further and rewrite the libretto entirely. In *¡Figaro!* *(90210)*, the writer Vid Guerrerio deftly updated the timeless storyline of Mozart's *Marriage of Figaro* to the twenty-first century, writing a brilliant English-Spanglish libretto that explores contemporary issues such as immigration. In this new version, Susanna and Figaro have become undocumented Mexicans working as a maid and handyman for Paul and Roxanne Conti, a Beverly Hills–based real estate mogul and aging actress (aka the Count and Countess). Mr. Conti, a hypocritical liberal, hints that he will help Susanna obtain a visa if she sleeps with him. The *droit du seigneur* that the Count ostensibly renounces in Mozart's original takes on an ominous contemporary twist that seems even more relevant after the avalanche of Hollywood sexual harassment scandals in late 2017. Guerrerio's contemporary take on the story—set to a chamber reduction of Mozart's original orchestral score—is a great example of how an opera can be deftly updated.

Although opera is still usually presented in the original language, a handful of companies, such as the Opera Theater of Saint Louis and the English National Opera, are presenting opera sung in English. Given the difficulty of understanding sung text, supertitles are usually provided even when the libretto is in the local language. The English National Opera began offering English supertitles in 2005 after surveys revealed that many listeners still struggled to comprehend the words (which provoked debates about the diction of modern singers compared to their predecessors). Even when rendered with razor-sharp clarity, a few words, particularly those sung by high voices, will inevitably remain unintelligible, and the denser the orchestration, the more likely some text will be missing in action. If the supertitles are to be used anyway, one might wonder why anyone would bother to present an opera sung in translation. One reason is simply to engage local audiences who might be more drawn to hearing a work sung in their mother tongue. For performances aimed at families, such as the Metropolitan Opera's holiday series, featuring the abridged *Magic Flute* and *Hansel and Gretel*—a wonderful opera by the German composer Engelbert Humperdinck— presenting in English translation makes sense.

The eighteenth-century English writer Dr. Samuel Johnson, who heard Italian opera in England, described opera as "an exotic and irrational entertainment which has always been combated, and always has prevailed." (As Johnson noted, despite the resistance, opera has always emerged victorious!) Composers and theaters have long made concessions to local listeners: in the nineteenth century, operas were often sung in the local language, but by the end of the twentieth they were mostly staged in their original languages. Some people deem opera an elitist art form in part because of this, but it seems an unfair accusation: a pop star who performs in a foreign idiom isn't considered exclusionary, so why is opera? In any event, with the advent of supertitles, language shouldn't be seen as a barrier, but savored as an integral part of the musical experience.

Indeed, while it can be rewarding to hear a comic opera or operetta performed in one's native language and colloquial vernacular, for the most part the idiosyncratic qualities of a particular language are part of the musical experience. Even audience members who don't understand a word can enjoy the crisp, sparkling sound of Italian, the sensual contours of French vowels, the luxuriant resonance of Russian sung by low voices, or the lilting, rounded sounds of Czech. There is also often something alluring about hearing singers perform in their native language. Listen to recordings of the late Dmitri Hvorostovsky, a remarkable Siberian baritone, singing the title role of *Eugene Onegin*, or Yeletsky's aria "Ya vas lyublyu" (I love you) from Tchaikovsky's *Queen of Spades*. The sonorities of Russian are integral to the sensual overall sound of this aria, and Hvorostovsky sings it with such innate musicality that it seems inconceivable that he should ever have sung it in any other language.

Each language poses specific hurdles for a composer. The British composer George Benjamin has discussed the challenges of composing to an English libretto:

> There's the vowels, open words, which are so good for high notes in the voice and so difficult to sing if you have a vowel like E—it's terrible to use in the high voice. There's consonants, and there's sibilance and the sounds of speaking, which are very suggestive and create great problems. "Create great problems"—the word "create" and "great" both have very loud vowels at the beginning: create, great. If I want to make a swooning, great

big legato lines, smooth line in the soprano part, and I had the words "create," "great" in the middle, I'd have to break the line. You can't go create, great—the mouth actually closes in order to get through the vowels, while other sentences will allow you to smoothly flow.

Music and text are intrinsically bound to each other in opera, and of course the same is true in popular music. The contours of Portuguese are part of the DNA of *fado* (a genre of blues), just as American English is integral to the music of Elvis Presley. It's hard to imagine Edith Piaf's "Non, je ne regrette rien" sung in English, or the Beatles' "Lucy in the Sky with Diamonds" in Chinese, just as it's hard to imagine *Peter Grimes* sung in Spanish. The way contemporary composers and librettists use language is an integral part of their operas, whether it's the English of John Adams's *Nixon in China*, the Sanskrit of Philip Glass's *Satyagraha*, the French of Kaija Saariaho's *L'Amour de Loin*, or the Quechua (an indigenous Peruvian language) briefly incorporated into Jimmy López's *Bel Canto*. Sung in any other language, these works would lose much in translation. The music of twenty-first-century opera is certainly a polyglot language and reflects a broad range of influences: there is no one sound or aesthetic that defines our multicultural, global era.

CHAPTER 6

ORPHEUS IN THE TWENTY-FIRST CENTURY

On contemporary opera, from Philip Glass to Kaija Saariaho

In the late eighteenth century, Italian academics fretted that opera was losing its noble roots and becoming a populist art form, while in the twentieth, authoritarian governments cracked down on operas deemed not populist enough. Listeners, performers, and composers have long wrestled with what constitutes the most effective musical language for sung drama—and composers have been accused throughout the centuries of being too cacophonous or too tuneful. Ascertaining what is "difficult" to listen to is, of course, entirely subjective, but more relevant than a composer's particular aesthetic is how effectively the musical language can convey a story. The same criteria that can be used to evaluate beloved operas of past centuries can be applied to new works. However traditional or avant-garde, the first decision for a composer and librettist has always been choosing a story. Why does a particular tale need music, and what will music add to it? How can music highlight the emotional journey of a character or the significance of a particular situation? How can the music underline and propel the drama, instead of merely accompanying it?

It's worth remembering that many now-beloved operas were abject failures at their premieres, while others received mixed receptions from critics and the public. Indeed, even some of the books that inspired contemporary operas—such as Melville's *Moby Dick* and Tolstoy's *Anna Karenina*—struggled at their inception. Conversely, many operas popular in the eighteenth and nineteenth centuries are now forgotten. In other words, it's impossible to predict what the "standard repertory" will be fifty years from now. With those disclaimers established, we'll explore examples of some of the most successful operas of recent decades, as well as a few that fell short.

Carmen, Violetta, and Tosca are unlikely to be dethroned anytime soon by Anna Karenina and Anna Nicole Smith, the heroines of recent operas. But there have been a remarkable number of new works written in the past few decades, even if many of them have not been staged more than once. According to OPERA America, 589 operatic works by North American composers premiered between 1995 and 2015 at companies in the United States and Canada; according to Operabase.com, there were 543 premieres worldwide between the 2011–2012 and 2015–2016 seasons. Many of the most successful recent operas have been inspired by films or novels, or have focused on contemporary topics, such as gay rights, terrorism, and capital punishment, often portraying significant figures from the political, cultural, sports, and celebrity spheres. Even Orpheus has resurfaced several times in recent years. There is no definitive twenty-first-century aesthetic: recent works include melodic and neo-romantic works, modernist operas with seemingly unsingable vocal lines, and works fusing elements of classical, pop, rock, jazz, and world music. There has even been a mariachi opera, José "Pepe" Martínez's *Cruzar la cara de la luna* (*To Cross the Face of the Moon*), a poignant story about immigrants.

Newcomers to opera may occasionally hear something and think "How can that possibly be an opera?" The definition of what constitutes opera continues to be challenged: some works now described as opera may lack plots, arias, or decipherable text—such as Helmut Lachenmann's *Das Mädchen mit den Schwefelhölzern* (*The Little Match Girl*). There's barely a complete sung sentence in the work, in which the orchestra conveys the mood of Hans Christian Andersen's tragic fairy tale with sounds effects that include whispers, gasps, bells, knocks, and cries. But if opera is defined as "sung drama," then how can something with almost no singing be classified as opera? Lachenmann's work, completed in 1996, was commissioned by the Hamburg State Opera, and, as Stephen Sondheim argued, whether something is classified as opera, musical theater, or some other genre depends partly on the venue presenting the piece. Listeners can hear the work on a recording and decide for themselves if they'd classify it as "opera."

Commentators weren't sure how exactly to classify

the first important opera of the modern era, Philip Glass's *Einstein on the Beach*, a five-hour work that shattered any previous templates into unrecognizable shards and broadened the parameters of what could be considered opera, although that wasn't Glass's intention. When asked in a 2013 interview whether he and the director, Robert Wilson, had set out to create an opera, Glass responded: "We wanted to do a proscenium piece, and we needed an orchestra pit. We needed fly space. We needed people who could sing. We needed people who could dance. You could call it anything you want to, but the only place we could do it was in an opera house."

Glass is one of the founders of *minimalism*—a genre that was in part a rebellion against the austere complexity of modernism. Minimalist music is rhythmically propulsive; it is based on the insistent repetition of short motifs and simple harmonies. It unfolds with a trance-like energy punctuated by harmonic and rhythmic shifts that signal changes in mood. Glass, who prefers the label "music with repetitive structures" to "minimalism," was born in 1937 in Baltimore and supported his fledgling compositional career as a young man by working as a plumber and a taxi driver. Early on, he transcribed *ragas* by the Indian sitarist Ravi Shankar into Western notation, and his exposure to Eastern forms of music had a profound effect on his own compositions. The musicians who perform raga—the term stems from the Sanskrit word for "passion" or "color"—aim to instill a spiritual mood in listeners, a trancelike state of mind that Glass's own music frequently precipitates. His aesthetic is familiar to many via his film soundtracks, which include *The Truman Show*, *The Hours*, and *Notes on a Scandal*.

Einstein both perplexed and awed listeners at the premiere in 1976 at the Metropolitan Opera. There was no intermission; instead, listeners were free to wander in and out as they pleased. In a review published that year in *The New Yorker*, the critic Andrew Porter wrote that a listener "usually reaches a point, quite early on, of rebellion at the needle-stuck-in-the-groove quality, but a minute or two later he realizes that the needle has not stuck; something has happened." In other words, if you can get in the groove, instead of feeling merely stuck in a groove, listening to the experimental *Einstein* can be a transcendent experience.

There is no discernible plot or coherent libretto in the opera, which is scored for amplified ensemble, a small chorus and soloists who sing and speak text consisting of numbers and solfège syllables. (In the solfège system a syllable is paired with each note of the scale. In the musical and film *The Sound of Music*, Maria uses the method to teach the Von Trapp children to sing.) Einstein's theories are alluded to via the manipulation of musical time, with an abstract, stream-of-consciousness libretto that includes enigmatic poems written by a young man with brain damage, numbers repeated in various sequences, and references to the Beatles, the pop song "Mr. Bojangles," and the trial of the heiress Patty Hearst. *Einstein* is divided into four acts, which are bridged with short connecting pieces that Glass called "Knee Plays." In Knee Play 1, the chorus intones the numbers from 1 through 8 over the drone of an electric organ and text uttered by two soloists, creating a surreal tapestry of sounds. The mood changes abruptly in the propulsive, breathless "Train," whose momentum is driven by the saxophone and keyboards. In a live performance, the character of Einstein is portrayed by a violinist, whose solos include the hypnotically beautiful Knee Play 2. (In real life Einstein played the violin. Check out the violinist Tim Fain's dazzling rendition of this interlude on YouTube.) The sense of existential angst that permeates the opera culminates in Act IV, with the relentlessly ascending and descending scales and frantic, soaring voices of "Spaceship" evoking a nuclear holocaust.

Glass's huge catalog also includes eleven symphonies, seven string quartets, some fifteen large-scale operas, and another dozen chamber opera and musical theater works. His best-known stage works are his so-called portrait operas—*Einstein on the Beach*, *Satyagraha* (about Mahatma Gandhi), and *Akhnaten* (about the Egyptian pharaoh), as well as large-scale stage works like *Appomattox* (about the concluding days of the American Civil War) and chamber operas such as *In the Penal Colony*—a riveting one-act work scored for string quartet and based on Franz Kafka's short story of the same name. The operas Glass wrote after *Einstein* and *Satyagraha* have largely adhered to a more conventional template and narrative-driven form.

Indeed, Glass wrote *Satyagraha* (his second opera) when the director of the Netherlands Opera asked him to write a "real" opera, and it premiered in 1980. It is scored for orchestra, chorus, and operatic voices and features traditional elements, including arias, but remains an avant-garde work despite these nods to convention. The libretto of

Satyagraha—from a Sanskrit word that translates roughly as "truth force"—was a collaboration between Glass and Constance DeJong and was inspired by the *Bhagavad Gita* (a Hindu scripture that is a colloquy between the Hindu god Krishna and the prince Arjuna that forms part of the epic *Mahabharata*). Although the text is drawn fully from this ancient source, the stage action explores Gandhi's life in South Africa between 1893 and 1914: the language and visuals together highlight (in nonchronological order) the evolution of his doctrine of nonviolent political protest and his efforts to enfranchise the country's Indian minority. The opera is sung in Sanskrit—another example of an opera in which the language of the libretto is crucial to the overall impact of the work. Glass stipulated that no supertitles be provided—he wanted listeners to hear the text but not understand it. However, for the marvelous coproduction between the Metropolitan Opera and the English National Opera, phrases and words translated into English were projected onto the stage as clues to the story.

The three acts of the opera are named after historical figures who appear as silent observers during staged productions: Tolstoy and the Bengali poet and anti-imperialist Rabindranath Tagore, who both inspired Gandhi, and Martin Luther King Jr., who was inspired by Gandhi. In the opening scene, the beautiful, mystical melody sung by the tenor portraying Gandhi unfolds above repeated patterns in the low strings, one of many moments where Glass's trademark repetitive figurations take on a poetic transcendence. The music for the "Confrontation and Rescue" scene in Act II is more turbulent: as Gandhi is followed by a mob through the streets, the chorus and orchestra convey his plight with ominous utterances and frantically spiraling motifs. The concluding scene of the opera is the most contemplative: Gandhi sings an ascending scale that repeats some thirty times, unfolding over ever-denser orchestral textures as the opera draws to a mystical close. Heard out of context, this passage might seem like something that could be titled "Revenge of the Broken Record," but for those who have immersed themselves in the whole opera, such repetitive passages, instead of grating on the nerves, take on a meditative intensity. Both *Einstein* and *Satyagraha* require a similar mindset from the listener: experiencing these operas is like watching a surrealist film or reading stream-of-consciousness prose.

GLASS'S DISTINCT MUSICAL LANGUAGE HAS HAD AN indelible impact on a generation of composers, including John Adams, born in 1947 in Massachusetts. Adams's first opera tells the story of Richard Nixon's meeting in China with Chairman Mao Zedong in 1972, following a twenty-five-year standoff between the United States and China. At the time when *Nixon in China* premiered at the Houston Grand Opera in 1987, it was unusual for an opera to feature characters based on living personalities and a story line inspired by a recent political event. The minimalist aesthetic is reflected in the simple ascending orchestral phrases that underline the chorus as they intone the "rules of discipline"—the doctrine Mao issued in 1928 for the

Red Army and China's peasants. In short, clipped phrases, the chorus sings:

> *Respect women, it is their due*
> *Replace doors when you leave a house*
> *Roll up straw matting after use*
> *The people are the heroes now.*

After Richard Nixon, First Lady Pat Nixon, and National Security Adviser Henry Kissinger touch down at the airport outside Peking and exchange pleasantries with Chinese officials, Nixon sings his "News Aria," in which he repeats the word "news" multiple times at the opening of the aria. The orchestra burbles and propels him along as he later sings: "We live in an unsettled time. / Who are our enemies? / Who are our friends?" He repeats the word "who" several times for emphasis.

The opera is both satirical and serious as it explores the cultural and philosophical issues of the historic meeting between the leaders of the capitalist and communist worlds. Neither man is portrayed as one-sided or a caricature; indeed, Adams said he wouldn't have chosen the subject matter if he hadn't thought he would be able to appreciate Nixon's humanity. In one interview, he said that a photo of Nixon crying after his wife's death reminded him that the former president "was a man who did have a heart, and he was capable of vision and humanity at the same time that he had a really dark and manipulative side."

Mason Bates, who composed *The (R)evolution of Steve Jobs*, which premiered at the Santa Fe Opera in 2017, took a similarly balanced outlook regarding his subject: after he received the libretto from Mark Campbell, Bates urged him to find more humanity in the characters. Campbell acknowledged that this decision to "neither deify nor demonize Steve Jobs, but to create a portrait of him as a human being," would attract criticism—which it did. But the opera, which incorporates Bates's trademark use of electronic and digital elements, is successful—in part because Jobs is not rendered a stock villain, even though the work's twenty nonchronological scenes explore the oft-cited dark elements of his personality, such as his unwillingness to acknowledge his illegitimate daughter and his mistreatment of colleagues.

While Adams took a risk in portraying a then living, real-life figure in *Nixon*, he faced far greater hurdles with the controversial *Death of Klinghoffer* (1991). Like *Nixon*, it has a libretto by Alice Goodman, an American writer who was raised in an observant Jewish household but converted to Christianity in adulthood, becoming an Anglican priest. Although Goodman did not complete another opera libretto after *Klinghoffer*, her contribution to contemporary opera is significant: her librettos are poetic, singable, and usually understandable without supertitles. The opera tells the true story of the death in 1985 of a Jewish American man, Leon Klinghoffer, who used a wheelchair (he had suffered two strokes): while vacationing with his wife, Marilyn Klinghoffer, on the *Achille Lauro* cruise ship, he was murdered by terrorists from the Palestine Liberation Front. Protests occurred at performances in 2014 at the Metropolitan Opera; some, including former New York mayor Rudy Giuliani, decried the opera because they believed it glorified the Palestinians as freedom fighters. Peter Gelb, the general manager of the Met, canceled a Live in HD broadcast owing to pressure from the Anti-Defamation League, which issued a statement saying that "while the opera itself is not anti-Semitic, there is a concern the opera could be used in foreign countries to stir up anti-Israel sentiments or as a vehicle to promote anti-Semitism." Klinghoffer's daughters have also vehemently opposed the opera, stating that it rationalizes and legitimizes the murder of their father. But Adams, who cut from the original version a controversial scene that was criticized for depicting an American Jewish household in a manner bordering on caricature, has said he wanted to condemn Klinghoffer's death and honor his memory while exploring the viewpoints of both Palestinians and Israelis. Some observers (including the placard-wielding protesters at Lincoln Center in 2014) criticized Adams for composing beautiful music for the terrorists, instead of accompanying them with the sinister or threatening music typically used for cinematic villains. In opera, however, bad guys often sing beautiful music.

The music is certainly alluring, beginning with the haunting "Chorus of Exiled Palestinians," in which a chorus of women sing with unemotive directness:

> *My father's house was razed*
> *In nineteen forty-eight*
> *When the Israelis passed*
> *Over our street.*

The emotional temperature heats up when the male voices join in, singing the words "Israel laid all to waste," with clipped, short syllables, and the chorus ends on a note of vengeance. The "Chorus of Exiled Jews" follows immediately afterward and unfolds with a simmering melancholy: "When I paid off the taxi, I had no money left, / and, of course, no luggage." It concludes with a gentle, lyrical line: "Your neighbor, the one who let me in, / she was brought up on stories of our love."

In a melismatic aria in Act I called "Now It Is Night," a terrorist, Mamoud, sings of how his brother and mother were killed in refugee camps; in Act II, Klinghoffer rebuffs him with an aria called "I've Never Been a Violent Man"— in which he sings,

> *Was it your pal*
> *Who shot that little girl*
> *At the airport in Rome?*
> *You would have done the same.*
> *There's so much anger in you*
>
> . . . .
>
> *You don't give a shit,*
> *Excuse me, about*
> *Your grandfather's hut,*
>
> . . . .
>
> *You just want to see*
> *People die.*

When at the end of Act II Marilyn Klinghoffer learns that her husband has been murdered, she sings: "They should have killed me. / I wanted to die." The opera ends on a note of quiet anguish.

Terrorists also sing beautiful music in *Bel Canto*, an opera by the Peruvian composer Jimmy López that premiered at the Lyric Opera of Chicago in December 2015. The work is based on Ann Patchett's popular 2001 novel of the same name, a fictionalized account of a real-life hostage situation that occurred in 1996, when the Túpac Amaru Revolutionary Movement attacked a gala party at the residence of the Japanese ambassador in Lima, Peru. The question of how music can add depth to a particular story is clear-cut when the story features an opera singer as a protagonist, and López aimed to imbue *Bel Canto* with the "heightened dramatic pacing" of cinema and musicals. Like the book, the opera explores the amorous relationships that develop between two couples: the hostages Roxanne Coss (a diva who has been hired to sing at the party) and Katsumi Hosokawa (a Japanese electronics CEO), and the guerrilla Carmen and Hosokawa's translator, Gen Watanabe. The opera features a polyglot libretto by Nilo Cruz, and the characters often perform in their native tongues: Carmen, for example, sings in an indigenous Peruvian language, Quechua. In ensemble scenes, the unique sonorities of the combined languages mesh into a multilingual blend that adds to the dramatic tension. At one point the guerrillas put a gun to Roxanne's head and force her to sing. She chooses a Handel aria, "Lascia ch'io pianga" (Let me weep), whose words—"Let me weep over / my cruel fate / and that I may sigh for freedom"—seem particularly resonant here. When Roxanne gives the guerrilla César a voice lesson, he sings "Una furtiva lagrima" (A furtive tear) from Donizetti's *L'elisir d'amore* (*The Elixir of Love*).

López uses leitmotifs and distinctive sound worlds for several characters, with percussion instruments, including glockenspiel and vibraphone, signaling the appearance of Joachim Messner (a Red Cross envoy). In his aria "Diplomacy," the vocal line evokes the melismatic singing of Monteverdi's Orfeo, an apt reference, because the modern envoy's rescue mission is similarly fraught. Monterverdi's *L'Orfeo* and the literary and operatic *Bel Canto* take root in the same premise: that beautiful singing can be a powerful instrument of communication, effective when the spoken word fails. As the tale of Orfeo, the singing musician of mythological lore, proved perfect fodder for the first successful opera, perhaps it should not come as a surprise that a book about the power of the human voice could offer similarly ripe material for a successful opera some four centuries later.

The guests are also trapped, albeit psychologically, not physically, in Thomas Adès's *The Exterminating Angel*, which received its premiere in 2016. Adès, a British composer who collaborated on the libretto with the director Tom Cairns, has described the "absence of will, of purpose, of action" that plagues the protagonists of the opera. He was inspired by Luis Buñuel's 1962 surrealist film *El ángel exterminador* (which has no musical soundtrack). In the opera, a dozen wealthy socialites are unable to motivate themselves to leave a dinner party even after most of the servants have fled, and the situation degenerates into a kind of aristocratic *Lord of the Flies*. The guests of the soirée, hosted by a high-society couple that has just seen a performance of *Lucia di Lammermoor*, include the opera singer Leticia, a doctor and patient, a conductor, a pianist, and an amorous young man and woman who commit suicide. The opera features a huge orchestra that includes Wagner tubas, miniature violins and cowbells, and the *ondes martenot*—an electronic instrument invented in 1928 that produces otherworldly sounds; it has been used by the Radiohead guitarist Jonny Greenwood as well as by several classical composers, including Olivier Messiaen. Adès uses it to aptly sinister effect in this opera to produce an eerie sound that represents the ghostly, unknowable force that prevents the dinner guests from leaving. The music evokes the societal decay unfolding: Viennese waltzes sound as if they've been reflected through a funhouse mirror, and melodic arias alternate with snippets of flamenco and polyphony in a densely woven score that reaffirms the composer's imagination and brilliance. Yet the opera is rarely particularly moving. The film, shot at close range, draws the viewer into the claustrophobic situation in a way that's difficult to replicate in a large opera house.

It's also hard to care about what happens to the characters, who can seem insufferable. Their angular vocal lines are often grating. Leticia sings in a piercingly high "Queen of the Night" range, which seems somewhat pointless and renders the sung English incomprehensible. Overall, the music adds little emotional depth to the film.

In her operatic version of the Lars von Trier film *Breaking the Waves* (1996), however, the American composer Missy Mazzoli added a vital, emotive dimension to the story. Like the cinematic *Exterminating Angel*, the Von Trier film has no musical soundtrack, providing

Mazzoli—who is sometimes described as "indie-classical" (a term for omnivorous twenty-first-century composers influenced by multiple genres)—with a blank canvas on which to illustrate the characters' emotional journeys. When the librettist Royce Vavrek suggested she turn the film into an opera, Mazzoli initially wondered whether it would be such a good idea, saying, "I thought it's such a brilliant film, so why mess with it? But the more I thought about it, the more I could hear a musical world that added a new dimension to the emotional landscape of the film."

The opera, which received its premiere in 2016 at Opera Philadelphia, hews closely to the plot of the film and its depiction of Bess McNeill, a member of an ultraconservative Calvinist sect living in a remote Scottish coastal village. Bess, a childlike and mentally unstable young woman, marries Jan, a Scandinavian oil-rig worker, but struggles when he leaves for the rig. She prays that he'll come home, but he returns in the most tragic circumstances after having been terribly injured in an accident on the rig. While paralyzed and incapacitated in the hospital, he urges her to have sexual relations with other men and then report back to him about the encounters. Bess is initially horrified by the idea, but she becomes convinced that if she follows his wishes, Jan will recover. Jan's health indeed improves, but Bess meets a tragic fate—she is gang-raped and dies from her injuries. Even in contemporary opera, women often meet a grisly fate—and yet both the librettist and the composer of *Breaking the Waves* clearly have the utmost respect for this character and the devastating choice she faces.

Whereas the filmmakers used shots of the dramatic Scottish landscape to enrich the narrative, Mazzoli's music—scored for a chamber orchestra, including an electric guitar, piano, strings, and brass—illuminates the emotional journeys of the protagonists. An all-male chorus depicts the mean-spirited Calvinist elders, with their curt, judgmental utterances serving as a startling contrast to Bess's soaring, lyrical lines. The male chorus also doubles as a group of oilmen who sing raucous music. In the midst of their singing, the brass instruments play phrases that swoop and shudder to convey the moment when the machinery falls on Jan with such chilling precision. The opera concludes with a climactic and musically ravishing scene of chorus and bells.

JUST AS SUPERB BOOKS ARE SOMETIMES TURNED INTO mediocre films, literary works and films don't always fare well as opera. Since a sentence that takes a few seconds to speak might take three times as long to sing, the challenge for the librettist is to condense what might be a complicated narrative into sung form. Ranieri Calzabigi, Gluck's librettist, elaborated one of the central problems of setting text to music when he wrote, "It is ridiculous to prolong the sentence 'I love you' (for instance) with a hundred notes when nature has restricted it to three." Several classic novels, including *The Scarlet Letter*, *The Grapes of Wrath*, *Anna Karenina*, and *Moby Dick*, have all been reincarnated in operatic form in recent years; Jake Heggie's *Moby Dick* was a popular and critical hit at its premiere at the Dallas Opera in 2010.

Gene Scheer, the librettist, omitted much of the whaling minutiae and nautical digressions from Herman Melville's novel and instead focused on the interactions between four characters—about half of the superb, tautly written libretto is taken directly from the novel. From the first notes of the sumptuous overture the score seethes with a dramatic tension that propels the drama forward. Ahab—the vengeful, crazed captain of the whaling ship *Pequod*—makes an immediate appearance, and soon afterward there is a riveting confrontation between Ahab and Starbuck, the voice of reason. When Ahab sings "Death to Moby Dick," his declaration is underscored by ominous orchestral swirls punctuated by drumbeats. The character of Ishmael has been renamed Greenhorn, and the role of narrator is taken on by the orchestra, whose undulating string lines evoke vast oceanic panoramas. There are nods to Philip Glass, Benjamin Britten, and Leonard Bernstein, as well as an echo of Giacomo Puccini in several voluptuous arias and duets. A stirring choral scene and tumultuous music of Wagnerian opulence conclude the opera.

Heggie's *Dead Man Walking* was a successful operatic take on a very different kind of book—the memoir of the same name by Sister Helen Prejean, a Catholic nun and prominent anti-death-penalty activist who wrote about her experience as spiritual adviser to death-row inmates at the Louisiana State Penitentiary. In the opera, which has a libretto by Terrence McNally—and has been frequently staged since its premiere in 2000 at the San Francisco

Opera—the protagonists' emotional journeys are brought to the fore, especially Sister Helen's, and her dilemmas about her role as confidante to people who have committed terrible crimes. The opera begins with a violent prologue depicting the rape and murder of teenage lovers by Joseph De Rocher, the man who will soon become Sister Helen's advisee. At her urging, he finally confesses and asks their parents for forgiveness. There are memorable ensemble scenes, such as when the bereaved parents berate Sister Helen; in the execution scene the voices of the warden, Joseph, Sister Helen, and family members of the murdered teenagers overlap in an emotional frenzy. The opera ends in near silence as a beeping sound (representing the convict's heart) fades away, signaling his death. This is followed by an a cappella reprise of the hymn "He Will Gather Us Around"—the leitmotif associated throughout the opera with Sister Helen.

Dead Man Walking turns a contemporary work of nonfiction into compelling sung drama, and the operatic *Moby Dick* successfully condenses a classic novel. The music of Robert Carlson's *Anna Karenina*, which premiered at the Florida Grand Opera in 2007, was less effective at conveying the emotional journey of the famous literary heroine. The librettist, Colin Graham (who died that year), focused on the love triangle between Anna, her husband, and Vronsky, as well as the love story between Kitty and Levin. He omitted some of the minor love stories and slightly altered the plot, although not as drastically as the classic films starring Vivien Leigh and Greta Garbo. Carlson is a deft orchestrator, and his lush, neo-romantic score incorporates colorful allusions to nineteenth-century Russia, like a version of the Czar's Hymn as a fate motif for Anna. Her mental decline is depicted with a vibraphone, and her death scene is compelling, with grittier music punctuated by loud bells. But overall, the music didn't add much depth to the story. In his review of the 2012 film starring Keira Knightley and Jude Law, the critic A. O. Scott wrote in the *New York Times* that "compressing the important events of Tolstoy's thousand pages into an impressively swift two hours and change, Mr. Wright turns a sweeping epic into a frantic and sublime opera." Both the film and the opera felt rather rushed: despite all the operatic potential of the literary Anna Karenina, her essence didn't quite translate to the stage.

While Carlson's soaring lyricism veers into saccharine territory in *Anna Karenina*, love sounds rather astringent in *Brokeback Mountain*, a chilly opera by the American modernist Charles Wuorinen. The opera is based on the short story of the same name by Annie Proulx about an ill-fated romance between two Wyoming ranch hands, Jack and Ennis, who meet in 1963 and continue their secret affair after marrying and having children. (The story also inspired the 2005 Oscar-winning film *Brokeback Mountain*.) The opera has a libretto by Proulx; it premiered in 2014 at the Teatro Real in Madrid. Although a tragic love story certainly doesn't have to be told with Puccini-like lyricism, the audience should of course feel moved, whatever the musical language. Wuorinen's orchestral music effectively conveys the harshness of the Wyoming landscape, and the simmering anger and violence of the story, but it rarely conveys passion or vulnerability. When Ennis admits to Jack that he is scared of his feelings and confused about why he feels drawn to Jack instead of his own wife, Alma, the amorous words seem at odds with the astringent vocal lines and the dour accompanying music, which renders the words heartless instead of heartbreaking. When Ennis sings that Jack has cured his loneliness, the music sounds detached and severe instead of hopeful. Just as the music and words of bel canto operas occasionally sound mismatched, the text and music here seem at odds. Harsh, even ugly, music can be used to thrilling effect in opera, as Strauss and Berg so brilliantly demonstrated in their depictions of insanity. But in tender moments a more expressive style is essential— otherwise, ostensibly loving words ring hollow.

The gay love affair of Gregory Spears's *Fellow Travelers* is depicted with much more emotional depth. The opera, based on the 2007 novel of the same name by Thomas Mallon, received its premiere at the Cincinnati Opera in June 2016, a week after the massacre of fifty people at a gay nightclub in Orlando, Florida. The book tells the fictional story of a romance between two men who have become caught up in the McCarthy era's "lavender scare," in which men and women suspected of being gay were persecuted. Following an executive order in 1953, thousands of people lost their jobs on grounds of "sexual perversion": they were deemed susceptible to blackmail and thus perceived as a security threat. When researching the novel, Mallon studied transcripts of the humiliating interrogations suffered by gay men and lesbians working in Washington, DC, during that era.

In the opera, the dashing Hawkins Fuller, a senior State Department official, is asked to walk across a room and take a lie detector test in which he will be questioned about his attraction to men. Timothy Laughlin, a shy, bespectacled, and piously Catholic recent college graduate and aspiring journalist, falls in love with Hawkins, who helps him get a job as a speechwriter. Eventually Tim joins the army in his attempt to recover from the ill-fated affair; Hawkins, meanwhile, marries a woman and betrays Tim to the government. The playwright Greg Pierce pared the book down to an efficient, conversational two-act libretto that focuses on the love affair, while retaining enough of the political drama to provide background to the story's setting. Fast-paced scenes flow cinematically and overlap seamlessly. Hawkins's poignant final aria, "Our Very Own Home," which was inspired by the troubadour songs of forbidden love, blends baroque and contemporary techniques. There are Wagnerian surges in the orchestra during a love scene between the two men at Tim's dingy apartment; lyrical arias, such as "Our Very Own Home" and "Last Night," are Puccini-like in their sweeping ardor. Crucially, the music adds depth to the drama and poignancy to the ill-fated affair.

THE WORD "ACCESSIBLE" IS SOMETIMES UNFAIRLY USED BY critics to imply that an opera is musically unsophisticated, but it certainly shouldn't be a pejorative. In the case of operas such as *Bel Canto* and *Fellow Travelers*, accessibility stems from the fast-paced action, gorgeous music, topical nature of the stories, and powerful emotions. When debating whether an opera will appeal to a wide audience or become a work for connoisseurs, the style of music is less relevant than the emotions it conveys and elicits. The modernist style of Berg's *Wozzeck* isn't easy listening; it's an "accessible" opera nonetheless because the music tells the story in a powerful and emotive way. The British composer George Benjamin's *Written on Skin* (2012) is arguably less accessible, because it's a much more subdued opera: despite a melodramatic story (which includes the suicide of yet another operatic heroine), its emotional temperature simmers but rarely boils until the final scenes. The opera has a libretto by Martin Crimp inspired by the life of the Catalan troubadour Guillem de Cabestaing, and it explores standard operatic issues—love, jealousy, fidelity, and betrayal.

The story follows the sexual awakening of a married woman (Agnès) with a young artist (the Boy) in medieval France. The Protector (Agnès's controlling husband) has hired the Boy to illustrate a manuscript celebrating the Protector's family. With its introduction of cannibalism to the opera stage, the opera surpasses even *Salome* in its gruesome conclusion. Benjamin is a masterful composer, and there are myriad alluring passages in the score, which includes the sounds of a typewriter, pebbles, *tabla* (South Asian hand drums), and the mandolin. But listening to the opera, which has fifteen scenes, is not a particularly involving experience: the passions of the story often seem subdued until scene 13, when, following a moment of deceptively ethereal music, the orchestra accompanies the final act of savagery with frantic string outbursts interwoven with brass interjections and a deadly crash of percussion.

The immaculately crafted music is stunning, the libretto poetic, and the vocal lines elegant, but it's an experience that's often more cerebral than moving. The same could also be said about *The Exterminating Angel*.

George Benjamin studied with Olivier Messiaen, a visionary French composer who experienced a form of synesthesia, whereby he interpreted certain sounds or harmonies as particular colors. Messiaen's rarely staged *St. François d'Assise* (*St. Francis of Assisi*), which received its premiere at the Paris Opera in 1983, certainly can't be included on the A-list of accessible operas, but it's worth listening to some of it via recording in order to appreciate his unique aesthetic. Messiaen, who died in 1992, was a devout Roman Catholic, and his faith deeply impacted his music. Many of his pieces have religious titles, such as the extraordinary piano work "Vingt Regards sur l'Enfant-Jésus" (Twenty Contemplations on the Baby Jesus). Messiaen spent much of his time in the countryside and was fascinated with birds. He would record and transcribe birdcalls, and for *St. François* he traveled to Assisi in Italy to transcribe the songs of local species. The five-hour-long opera is written for an orchestra of some 120 musicians and a choir of 150 singers. The choir acts as a Greek chorus and divine commentator. The three acts are divided into eight scenes and set in thirteenth-century Italy. The opera highlights the spiritual journey of the title character, including his embrace of a leper and his ecstatic death. Messiaen wrote the libretto himself, basing it on St. Francis's writings and prayers, as well as biblical passages and scholarly records of the saint's life.

The opera is a bird of Wagnerian plumage, with rumi-
native vocal lines that can become ponderous, and that at
times require a saintly patience from listeners. But the choral and orchestral music of *St. François* is often startlingly
beautiful, with themes played on different instruments to
reflect the mood and psychological development of each
scene. Leitmotifs accompany each character: for Francis,
an evocative theme in the strings descends and rises with
questioning insistence. An extraordinary passage in Act II,
scene 5, "L'ange musicien" (Angel musician), was inspired
by the moment in Franciscan hagiography when an angel plays an exquisite melody on the viol to offer Francis
a glimpse of celestial delights; in the opera, the ethereal
tune is rendered with haunting delicacy by the ondes martenot. In scene 6 Francis preaches to the birds, and Act II
concludes with an avian extravaganza in the riotous Grand
Concert of the Birds. "Lord! Music and poetry have led me
to Thee," sings Francis in the finale of Act III, before dying. The opera finishes with an ecstatic Resurrection chorus
and a kaleidoscopic tumult of birdsong.

Messiaen's grand opera inspired Kaija Saariaho, a
prominent Paris-based Finnish composer, to write *L'Amour
de loin* (*Love from Afar*). In 2016, it was only the second
opera by a woman presented by the Metropolitan Opera;
it came more than a century after Ethel Smyth's 1903 *Der
Wald*, the first opera by a woman shown at the Met. Indeed,
while women composers, conductors, and directors have
certainly made strides in recent years, opera is still largely a
man's world: the Metropolitan Opera's 2017–2018 season,
for example, included no female composers or conductors;

nor were any scheduled for the 2018–2019 season. The first known opera by a woman is Francesca Caccini's comic *La liberazione di Ruggiero dall'isola d'Alcina* (*The Liberation of Ruggiero from the Island of Alcina*), which was based on the epic poem *Orlando furioso* (which also inspired some of the operas by Handel discussed in Chapter 1). It was performed in 1625 in Florence.

Saariaho has said that listening to music should be a sensual experience, which this opera certainly is—one that feels more akin to *Tristan and Isolde* and *St. François d'Assise*—operas that focus on the characters' inner worlds—than to narrative-driven operas like *Carmen* or *La traviata*. Saariaho's opera, which has a poetic libretto by her frequent collaborator Amin Maalouf, follows the story of Jaufré Rudel, a medieval French prince-troubadour who is bored of his hedonistic lifestyle and hopes to find a perfect woman. He is shocked to discover that she actually exists: Clémence, the faraway Countess of Tripoli. Even without having seen her, Jaufré is immediately smitten; the Countess, on the other hand, is skeptical when she learns about Jaufré. The troubadour travels to meet her and they declare their love, but he dies in her arms. She decides to move to a convent—a place where surviving operatic heroines often end up. Saariaho blends electronic and acoustic elements to scintillating effect in her music, and the theatricality of the opera's iridescent score—with its soaring vocal lines and luxuriant choruses, as well as its contrast between dramatic surges and simmering hazes—compensates for the lack of onstage action.

In many of the operas thus far discussed, the composers and librettists seem to sympathize with the protagonists to some degree, or at the very least tried to find some humanity in even the most flawed characters. This is not so in the opera *Anna Nicole*, by the British composer Marc-Anthony Turnage. This work, inspired by the tragic life of the *Playboy* model and playmate Anna Nicole Smith, who became a focus of controversy when she married the octogenarian billionaire J. Howard Marshall, was marred by its condescending depiction of the title character. When the opera received its premiere in 2011 at the Royal Opera House in London, the organization posted a warning on its website about "extreme language, drug abuse and sexual content." That wasn't what they should have been concerned about, however. The satirical opera, a deft blend of classical, rock, jazz, and blues, certainly has its share of entertaining moments, but the characters, in particular Anna Nicole, are caricatures. In an interview in 2013 with *New York* magazine, Turnage acknowledged that he had some regrets: "If I'm really honest, I'm quite uncomfortable with it now....I don't think we were trying to be cruel. But it's mocking someone's real life. I wouldn't do it again." Anna Nicole died at the age of thirty-nine of a drug overdose.

A fallen woman is also ridiculed in Thomas Adès's tragicomic opera *Powder Her Face*, a youthful work with a libretto by Philip Hensher that tells the story of the Lulu-like Duchess of Argyll, whose sexual escapades during her scandalous divorce made headlines in Britain in the 1960s. Like *Anna Nicole*, *Powder Her Face* is often entertaining and musically witty. It's notorious for its so-called *fellatio aria*. But the scornful depiction of the Duchess is problematic—although a talented performer may succeed in imbuing the character with a semblance of dignity. The audience does get a moment to pity the unlikable Duchess in Act II, when she is presented with an enormous hotel bill: her anguish as she digests the numbers is echoed by deflated orchestral sounds that slither downward in a gesture of defeat, and when her voice becomes more agitated, the orchestra echoes her in a crescendo of despair. The music is stark and spare in the following scene as the hotel manager tells her she must vacate the hotel she has long occupied. At the end of the aria "Servants Used to Know When to Go," the Duchess mournfully sings, "And there's no one to dress me, and no one to talk to me. / And the only people who were ever good to me were paid for it." The orchestral music sounds funereal. She then breaks an empty perfume bottle against the wall in a mad scene that cements her downfall: during her humiliating eviction, there is none of the glib musical irony of the earlier scenes. In her final aria, she implores the hotel manager to hold her and sit by her and begs, unsuccessfully, for his patience. But our sympathy evaporates soon after: the libretto stipulates that "she makes a blatant assault on him," and the opera ends on a farcical note, with frenetic tango music accompanying a romp between hotel staff. The opera would have been more powerful if it had ended on a note of empathy instead of mockery.

The American composer Robert Ashley, who died in 2014 at the age of eighty-three, found the humanity in ordinary folk—but his ordinary folk often have dramatic secrets. His operas are a sort of contemporary verismo in which mundane events become surreal. He seamlessly meshes narrative threads about quotidian events with contemplations about life, aging, religion, and love. The voices of multiple speakers deliver texts (sometimes simultaneously) with subtle, melodic cadences that become a colorful vocal tapestry. The beauty of Ashley's works lies in the way his half-sung lines become music, with mundane happenings taking on an otherworldly hue. In a 2001 interview with *NewMusicBox*, Ashley said he had been inspired more by the Beach Boys and Chuck Berry than by Puccini or Wagner; he thought some elements of operatic singing, such as the elongation and ornamentation of vowels, were ill suited to American English. Like other pioneers, such as Philip Glass, Ashley further broadened the scope of what could be considered opera. He set the text in his operas in such a way that the words are crystal clear in solo monologues, but closer to a stream of consciousness than a linear narrative. His setting of text resembles German *Sprechstimme*—the style in which words are intoned more musically than in regular speech, but stop short of song. "It is foolish to argue that opera—any opera—can have a plot," he said. "That is, that the 'characters' and their apparent 'actions' and the apparent 'consequences' are related in any way. Opera can be story-telling only."

Ashley's stories unfold in meditative, intimate digressions, with electronic scores that sometimes evolve live during a performance to reflect the idiosyncrasies of particular singers. *The Trial of Anne Opie Wehrer and Unknown Accomplices for Crimes Against Humanity* (1968) is sometimes referred to as a "speaking opera." Two characters pose questions, ranging from mundane inquiries about dates and names to quirkier queries, such as "Please describe the most insignificant thing you've done with your hair," and "Can you learn from your past?" In an almost two-hour, uninterrupted "interrogation," the questions and answers ebb and flow with steady insistence, answers to one question sometimes unfolding over a consecutive query. Ashley thought television was an ideal medium for opera, in part because of its intimacy and speed; his attraction to television was a direct repudiation of operatic tradition, which he thought had little relevance for a contemporary American audience. Television, he told the author Kyle Gann, is the most suitable medium for opera. "I put my pieces in television format because I believe that's really the only possibility for music," he said. "The form is related to the architecture. La Scala's architecture doesn't *mean* anything to us. We don't go there. We stay at home and watch television."

Ashley's television opera *Perfect Lives*—a story set in the American Midwest, featuring a bank robbery, teenage love, and cocktail lounges—was broadcast by Channel 4 in London in 1983 in seven video segments of about thirty minutes each. *Vidas Perfectas*, a Spanish-language incarnation of *Perfect Lives*, was transposed to the US-Mexican border. Ashley's operas are widely available on YouTube, a medium of viewing—far from La Scala—that he would no doubt have approved of. Indeed, opera is now widely accessible online, and chances are that any websurfer who would like to hear a particular singer's interpretation of a certain aria will be able to find it on YouTube and compare it to performances by many other singers.

The aforementioned works, for all their admirable qualities, aren't exactly a barrel of laughs. In light of so many new operas ending with cannibalism, rape, death row, or the nunnery, an opera buff may well wonder whether composers have lost their sense of humor. There have been only a handful of genuine comedies in recent decades, including a hilarious musical incarnation of Oscar Wilde's *The Importance of Being Earnest* (2010), by the Irish composer Gerald Barry. Barry cut the play substantially and created a witty, pungent, and maniacal score with cacophonous outbursts (including dissonant remakes of "Auld Lang Syne"), angular, zigzagging vocal lines, and comic musical wit that add even more pungency to Wilde's play. The libretto (based largely on Wilde's original text) is accompanied by impertinent squeaks from the woodwinds, indecent outbursts from the brass section, and—at one point—the smashing of dozens of plates.

But while contemporary composers have mostly chosen grim topics for their operas, there have been new stagings of old works offering plenty of opportunity, albeit at times inopportune, for laughter. There is enormous variety in the way opera is now staged, with much depending on the venue and the director. Minimalist and sumptuous, G-rated and R-rated, logical and bizarre, traditional and outlandish: it seems that anything goes on the opera stage in the twenty-first century. In the next chapter we'll discuss what opera-goers might expect to see when they attend a staged production, and how different directors can have startlingly different interpretations of the same opera.

CHAPTER 7

APE COSTUMES OR PERIOD COSTUMES?

ON STAGING OPERA IN THE TWENTY-FIRST CENTURY

IN ACT II OF PUCCINI'S *TOSCA*, THE LIBRETTO STIPULATES that after the title character murders the police chief, Baron Scarpia, she should place a crucifix on his chest and one candle on either side of his body, actions that take place during a simmering orchestral postlude. There were howls from the cognoscenti when the director of the Metropolitan Opera's 2009 production, Luc Bondy, did not include these symbolic gestures in his staging. Some viewers seemed more irked by this deviation from tradition than by the addition of a graphic orgy between Scarpia and three voluptuous prostitutes earlier in Act II. Bondy, a Swiss-born director who died in 2015, was well respected in Europe, where salacious touches and provocative concepts are more routine than in the United States. He responded to the hubbub by saying, during a panel discussion at the

New York Public Library in 2009, "I was scandalized that they were so scandalized. I didn't know that *Tosca* was like the Bible in New York."

Since *Tosca* has long been part of the standard repertory, along with other audience favorites, such as *Carmen*, *La bohème*, and *La traviata*, an opera buff of a certain age might have seen *Tosca* dozens of times in the theater, but attend yet another performance to hear a particular singer or see a new staging. That could range from a traditional production that keeps the story intact, featuring period costumes and sets, to one that looks more modern, updating the story to a different era but without making drastic changes to the plot or characters. The latter type of production can look modern but remain essentially traditional. Further along on that end of the spectrum, however, is *Regietheater*, German for "director's theater," radical and sometimes outlandish reinterpretations that might pay little heed to the original creators' intentions.

Indeed, Bondy's transgression of the missing crucifix and candles certainly seems meek when compared to *Regietheater*, which is sometimes less politely called Eurotrash. In *Regietheater*, the director's vision (or lack thereof) is paramount, sometimes to the detriment of the music, plot, and singing. Some stagings have been gratuitously weird, such as a 2005 production of *Rigoletto* for the Bavarian State Opera. The avant-garde German film director Doris Dörrie was inspired by *Planet of the Apes* and *Star Wars*, and thus, according to a review in the *Financial Times* by the critic Shirley Apthorp, the Duke of Mantua wore a gorilla costume, and Rigoletto a space suit. Gilda

was a Princess Leia lookalike. Some of the smaller characters, wrote Apthorp, were depicted as "simian creatures,
hunched, hairy and horny, humping lampposts and eating
each other's fleas as the planets turn above." Opera in Europe is still primarily funded by public and government
money, whereas in the United States funding is mostly
from private donors and foundations. Audiences tend to
be more conservative in America, and companies sometimes take fewer risks to avoid offending both donors and
subscribers.

Operatic orangutans were certainly a peculiar choice
for *Rigoletto*; other directors have offered productions that
are less zany. In 2002, the Welsh National Opera set the
story in the Kennedy-era White House. The Duke was a
Hollywood studio boss in a 2000 Los Angeles Opera staging, and in the Metropolitan Opera's 2013 production, the
action takes place in Rat Pack–era Las Vegas. There's certainly a happy medium between period costumes and ape
costumes.

In its 2017–2018 season, the Metropolitan Opera returned to tradition with a production of *Tosca* by the Brit-
tish director David McVicar that dutifully included the
requisite candles and crucifix. Until 2009, the Met used
the Italian director Franco Zeffirelli's 1985 staging of the
opera, which had featured sumptuous, richly detailed sets
and costumes. Zeffirelli productions are a spectacle—in his
1981 staging of *La bohème*, which is still a crowd-pleaser
at the Met, the audience invariably applauds heartily as
the curtain goes up during the Café Momus scene. Zeffirelli's opera-as-spectacle aesthetic has a long history dating

back to the productions in the theaters of seventeenth-century Venice, which were often spectacularly lavish. One observer who experienced Francesco Manelli's *Andromeda* at Venice's Teatro San Cassiano in 1637 raved in his memoir about the "marvelous transformation scenes, the crowded stage, the ingenious mechanism, the flying figures, the scenery representing the heavens, Olympus, the ocean, royal palaces, forests, groves, and innumerable other enchanting spectacles." Those eye-popping stagings, in turn, took root from the *intermedi*, the lavish sixteenth- and seventeenth-century entertainments performed to honor royal weddings and births as well as important state events. A description of one *intermedio*, staged during festivities held in 1589 to celebrate the wedding of a member of the Medici family, noted "the two winged dragons which stuck out their tongues, spewing flames," a sorceress who appeared on a golden chariot decorated with precious stones, and the moment when "the stage was covered with fiery rocks, chasms and caverns, from which flames leapt and smoke billowed up."

There's nothing wrong with a good spectacle—and it's fun to watch a sumptuous production of *Aida* with a lavish triumphal scene—but it becomes problematic when the scenery literally dwarfs the singers. The Café Momus scene in *La bohème* is described in the libretto as a "vast and motley crowd of citizens, soldiers, serving girls, children, students, seamstresses, gendarmes, etc." Zeffirelli faithfully evoked that bedlam with nineteenth-century postcard realism: jugglers entertain a crowd of children onstage, and townspeople swarm every which way. It's entertaining to watch, but there's a "Where's Waldo?" element to it all: the main characters, submerged in the swirling crowds, seem physically and vocally diminished. The Act II soirée in Zeffirelli's production of *La traviata* at the Metropolitan Opera was similarly claustrophobic—a visual cacophony of glitter, streamers, and lavish decor.

After retiring Zeffirelli's overwrought production of *La traviata*, the Met offered an elegantly modern, minimalist staging by the German director Willy Decker. His version had originated at the Salzburg Festival in 2005 and starred Anna Netrebko in a charismatic performance as Violetta. In Decker's bare, abstract staging, a curved wall looming over the stage forms an ominous backdrop throughout the opera. A large ticking clock on one side of the stage hints at Violetta's imminent demise, and her bright red cocktail dress and a red sofa provide a splash of color in the austere surroundings. The male and female partygoers, all dressed alike in black tuxedos, become a creepy, androgynous mob crowding around her; they seem to nearly suffocate her (both literally and figuratively). At other times, the hostile mob leers from above the wall in mocking judgment. Dr. Grenvil, meanwhile, lurks silently as a sort of grim reaper. In Act II, a swath of florid fabric is draped over the clock, as if giving Violetta and Alfredo a brief free moment of domestic happiness in the countryside. Crucially, in this bleak but beautiful staging the intimate drama rightfully takes precedence over the scenery, whereas in Zeffirelli's production, it was the other way around. Decker's *La traviata* is an example of modern production at its best: it is visually striking, psychologically meaningful, and dramatically effective.

THE SAME OPERA CAN BE INTERPRETED BY DIFFERENT directors in ways that radically alter our perceptions of the story. David McVicar brought an imaginative, lighthearted touch to his production of Handel's *Giulio Cesare*, which debuted at the 2005 Glyndebourne Festival in England. Caesar and the Roman conquerors are depicted as nineteenth-century British officers, and the Egyptians as Indians, Middle Easterners, and others colonized by British rule. Clad in bright red jackets and carrying small trunks, the British soldiers march onto the stage during the opening choral number, which celebrates Caesar in a jubilant Bollywood-style take on the opera. Handel's vocal lines are surprisingly well suited to Bollywood dance moves. In her aria "Da tempeste il legno infranto" (When the ship, broken by storms), Cleopatra wears breeches and boots, and two dancers mimic her moves. The colorful staging is witty and entertaining—it is successful because camp is judiciously balanced with the pathos inherent (and essential) to the story. When Caesar is presented with Pompeo's head, for example, the soldiers stand still as Caesar fumes against Tolomeo's cruelty; Cornelia and Sesto weep in the background. When Sesto swears vengeance, he is alone on stage; his anger and grief are not hindered by distracting onstage antics. Thus, in spite of the Bollywood moves, it was a less radical production than Lydia Steier's 2015 version for the Komische Oper Berlin, which added gratuitous elements such as incest to the story. Updating the setting to the colonial era, as McVicar did, made sense, but the ambiguous Handelian setting of Steier's production, which featured decaying aristocratic mansions, along with hordes of cavorting aristocrats wearing outfits evoking a baroque fetish costume party, offered little insight. The strangest directorial choice—and one that inadvertently seemed to torture both performer and listener—was casting a baritone as Caesar. Handel wrote the title role, which requires enormous coloratura skill, for a castrato, and it's now typically sung by countertenors and mezzo-sopranos. Since there are many singers with the vocal chops for this athletic role, casting a baritone with an inflexible voice seemed cruel. Just as viewers should question how a directorial choice offers new insight into the story, they should also ask what a particular voice brings to a role.

Operas like Bizet's *Carmen* are often staged with folkloric kitsch, swirling skirts, and fringe shawls, but the Catalan director Calixto Bieito avoided castanet clichés in his production, updating the setting from Seville to 1970s Spanish North Africa. Bieito, who has been called "the Quentin Tarantino of opera," has earned notoriety for his provocative productions. His staging of Verdi's *Ballo in maschera* (*A Masked Ball*) for the English National Opera, for example, opened with the male chorus sitting on a row of toilets (trousers at their ankles). Much of Bieito's well-traveled production of *Carmen* is similarly stripped down. When a gun-toting solider wearing only his skivvies runs laps around his fully attired comrades, it seems as if he is being humiliated for some transgression, an image that evokes male sadism—and the male aggression confronting Carmen. A nude matador might seem gratuitous, but in this staging it's not: the scene was inspired by the "moon baptism," a bullfighter tradition in which first-time matadors practice a ritual with the bulls under a full moon. Other of Bieito's ideas are more debatable. Bizet, for example, depicts Micaëla as the virtuous girl-next-door, but in Bieito's version she becomes a flirt. One of the most potent moments is during the finale, which in many productions is a crowded scene. But in Bieito's version the stage is empty: we are alone with Don José and Carmen in their final moments. This choice renders the drama more acute than when they are surrounded by hordes of gaping onlookers. Bieito's *Carmen* is an example of a boundary-testing production that makes sense—but his staging for the Komische Oper Berlin of Mozart's *Abduction from the Seraglio* earned him a reputation for pushing the envelope too far. The opera is usually plumbed for its comic elements, but Bieito updated its Turkish harem to a modern-day brothel filled with victims of sex trafficking (one of whom is murdered and has her nipple slashed off).

Graphic depictions of sexual violence are unfortunately too prevalent in contemporary opera stagings. A 2015 production of Rossini's *Guillaume Tell* at the Royal Opera House in London by the Italian director Damiano Michieletto updated the setting to the Bosnian conflict of the 1990s. It was heavily criticized for a rape scene in which an anonymous female member of the chorus was stripped naked and assaulted by officers. Reviewers criticized the scene not only for its gratuitous violence but because it contradicted the character of the music itself.

The relationship between the sexes is an integral part of opera, and how to interpret those dynamics is one challenge facing directors. When Leporello berates Don Giovanni for assaulting Donna Anna and murdering her father, English translations and supertitles sometimes render the phrase "sforzar la figlia" as "ravish the daughter." The archaic meaning of the verb "to ravish" is to abduct or rape, but in a contemporary context, "ravish" often has a more positive connotation. Thus, upon learning that Giovanni has "ravished" a woman, someone might at first assume it was a welcome encounter. The libretto itself doesn't reveal exactly what transpires in Donna Anna's bedroom in the first scene, but it seems safe to assume that since she screams, it isn't a welcome encounter. "Sforzar la figlia" is also sometimes translated as "seduce the daughter," but a more fitting translation is "force himself on the daughter," or "rape the daughter."

Throughout the opera, Mozart's music reveals little about the title character, so how we perceive Giovanni depends largely on how the opera is staged and sung. Some directors highlight comic elements, such as the wry words of Leporello, the buffa character. But there are few opportunities for laughs in Peter Sellars's version of the opera, which he set on the mean streets of a South Bronx neighborhood during the crack epidemic, a landmark production broadcast on public television in 1990. Sellars, an American director born in 1957, made headlines in the 1980s for his revolutionary productions of the Mozart–Da Ponte trilogy—he set *The Marriage of Figaro* in Trump Tower in Manhattan, and *Così fan tutte* in a diner run by a Vietnam War veteran. Sellars takes an unequivocal stance about Giovanni, deeming him no mere rascally womanizer: "Sforzar la figlia" is translated in the subtitles as "Rape the daughter." In the first scene, we see Donna Anna disheveled and struggling to escape Giovanni's clutches. She has large, bloody scratch marks on her chest. "Donna folle! Indarno gridi!" (Foolish woman! Your screams are in vain!), sings Giovanni, later pulling her up by her hair. When he tells her she will never discover his identity, his admonitions are translated in this production as: "Shut up bitch, you'll never find out who I am."

Michael Grandage's 2011 production for the Metropolitan Opera is bland by comparison. With an unimaginative staging, period costumes, dreary sets, and a mid-eighteenth-century Spanish locale—it offers less of an indictment of Giovanni. Donna Anna emerges from her quarters in a tidy white nightgown and robe, her hair and clothes unrumpled. She's irate, certainly, but doesn't appear to be struggling too much as Giovanni runs his hands all over her body. After Giovanni stabs the Commendatore (her father), he gently lowers the dying man to the ground, whereas in the Sellars production, Giovanni is a psychopath—he lights up a joint immediately after shooting the Commendatore in the stomach.

For the filmed production, Sellars cast identical twins (Eugene Perry, a baritone, and Herbert Perry, a bass-baritone) as Giovanni and Leporello. In a typical staging, Leporello's remonstrations against his master often garner chuckles from the audience, but in Sellars's South Bronx setting there's not much to giggle about in the "Catalogue Aria": Leporello sings it standing ominously close to Elvira, snapping his fingers with sinister emphasis as he tallies up his master's conquests. It's a much less ominous scene in the Grandage production: here, ladies appear coyly at the balcony windows as Leporello sings the aria.

In a rare moment of humor in the Sellars staging, Leporello turns on a boom box and plays tunes popular in Mozart's era. He then looks away in disgust as his master eats a McDonald's meal on the stoop, during what is usually staged as a formal banquet scene. As radical a directorial point of view as this may seem, it works. At no point is the story or the music compromised, and viewers are not distracted from the music by trying to figure out what's going on.

Roland Schwab's quirky 2010 production of *Don Giovanni* for Deutsche Oper Berlin, in contrast, had some extremely distracting elements. The setting was updated to what looked like a nightclub scene, in theory a viable concept for an opera about a man who likes to womanize and party. But what did the entourage of men in business suits waving golf clubs symbolize? Were the women wrapped in cellophane lying prostrate on a red-lit rotating contraption supposed to be Giovanni's victims? Why did a woman with a prosthetic leg wander across the stage? What about the man—who appeared to be Jesus—pedaling away on a stationary bicycle at the side of the stage? None of it made much sense. The trouble with such stagings is that they add little insight to the story and end up taking our attention away from the singing. The plot twists of opera can be complicated enough without having to figure out why someone is dressed like Jesus, or wearing an ape costume, or hanging upside down from the ceiling.

The best stagings are noteworthy for their insights rather than their oddities. The French theater director Patrice Chéreau (who died in 2013) made his name in the opera world in 1976 with a groundbreaking centennial staging at Bayreuth of the Ring Cycle. Chéreau updated the setting to the industrial revolution and featured a hydroelectric dam instead of the Rhine. He depicted the Rhinemaidens as nineteenth-century prostitutes, the giants as peasants, and the gods as members of a doomed aristocracy. (Alberich is a mean-spirited factory owner, and Wotan an ambitious entrepreneur.) Not everyone immediately appreciated Chéreau's production—it was booed during its opening run at Bayreuth—but it gained increasing favor in succeeding years and is now accepted as a landmark staging. Chéreau's use of the myths and legends of the opera to critique capitalist society was an apt interpretation of Wagner's epic cycle about power, greed, and corruption.

Other directors of the Ring Cycle have chosen to avoid any kind of "interpretation," instead focusing on naturalistic stagings. Otto Schenk did this in his old-fashioned production for the Metropolitan Opera that ran between 1986 and 2011. "I avoided interpretations," he said in an interview with the *Washington Post* in 2009. "I think when it says it's set in a forest, I want to see a forest, and when it's set in a cave, I want to see a cave. My imagination is limited. I can't imagine that an empty platform is a forest." There were also old-fashioned elements in Robert Lepage's production for the Met, which replaced the Schenk staging, but similarly took no particular point of view. Lepage was not interested in sociopolitical interpretations—his version became known instead for a hulking forty-five-ton contraption that dominated the stage. Consisting of twenty-four rotating planks, it came to be referred to as

"The Machine": the mechanical beast generated more discussion than any of the gods, dragons, or giants of the story. Its moving parts often malfunctioned, distracting the audience from elements of the opera that were more visually alluring, such as the striking digital images featured in many scenes.

A staging by the American director Francesca Zambello, presented most recently at the Washington National Opera in 2016, proved both visually stunning and psychologically insightful, however. The production has been described as an "American Ring." *Das Rheingold* is set in Gold Rush–era California, where Alberich is panning for gold. As the cycle unfolds, the environmental purity of the nineteenth-century American West degenerates into widespread ecological destruction, and the gods' fight to maintain their power becomes a metaphor for the struggle between the one percent and the economic underclass. The Nibelungs are portrayed as suffering workers instead of manipulative dwarves. Wotan is a greedy businessman who signs shady real estate deals, presiding over his empire from a Manhattan skyscraper. At the end of this *Das Rheingold*, the gods, dressed in early twentieth-century finery, ascend to Valhalla via the gangplank of a ship that could be the doomed *Titanic*. In Act II of *Die Walküre*, Siegmund and Sieglinde flee the wrathful Hunding and take shelter under a decaying interstate overpass. *Siegfried* takes place in a desolate landscape in which a grimy trailer is parked near a trash heap and a decaying power plant; in *Götterdämmerung*, the Rhinemaidens see their river polluted and destroyed.

In addition to presenting ecological allegories of contemporary society, this version is also a rare (even unique) feminist take on the Ring Cycle. Both the gods and the mortals are flawed: the only unblemished character—and the real hero of the cycle—is Brünnhilde, who saves a world that has been wrecked by men. During the "Ride of the Valkyries," the singers parachute onto the stage dressed as Amelia Earhart–style fighter pilots. According to Zambello, "Specifically now, what resonates is that so much of the Ring from Wagner's perspective is about the destruction of nature but also the birth and rebirth of nature. Even more than five years ago, the connections of the work and Wagner's words of warning to our belated grasping of global warming. Greed destroys not just nature but the natural order, and it takes a woman to set things right again."

IN 1888, TCHAIKOVSKY WROTE IN HIS DIARY THAT HE HAD "never encountered anything more false and foolish than the effort to get truth into opera. In opera everything is based upon the not-true." Which means that a fifty-year-old might be convincing as a teenage consumptive, or a portly middle-aged man as an ardent young lover. If the "truth" lies in the emotions the singer conveys with his or her voice, then it really doesn't matter what the singer looks like. Sometimes viewers aren't willing to suspend disbelief, however. At the premiere of *La traviata* in 1853, the audience jeered the soprano Fanny Salvini-Donatelli, an ample thirty-eight-year-old—they weren't buying the idea that she could be a fragile young woman dying of consumption. Strauss was unsure about casting a popular Dresden soprano of stout girth as the teenager Salome; he concluded that the fact that she could handle the vocal challenges was ultimately more important than her looks.

Opera singers now face the same pressures as most other performing artists to be slim and attractive, and they are certainly under more pressure than ever to "look the part," even if visual realism is less important in opera than in other genres, such as theater or cinema. The American soprano Deborah Voigt was fired in 2004 from the title role in a production of Strauss's *Ariadne auf Naxos* (*Ariadne on Naxos*)—then one of her signature parts—because she was unable to wear the slinky dress envisioned by the casting director. After this episode, which became known as the Little Black Dress saga, Voigt underwent gastric bypass surgery. There have certainly been other productions that have featured cocktail dresses suitable only for a slender singer: it's presumably not a coincidence that only slim sopranos have been hired to sing Violetta in Decker's *La traviata*, for example. The character always wears a fitted knee-length cocktail dress.

The debate about how realistic a singer should look in a role has grown more pressing given that opera is now often experienced through multiple visual platforms, including the Live in HD series. Opera has long been shown on television and DVD, but clearly, on a big screen in a cinema, the visual elements come into even sharper focus. On radio broadcasts or recordings, the experience is solely about the voice, and audience members watching from a seat in a theater far from the stage aren't going to see many visual details unless they've brought binoculars. But in a Live in HD broadcast, when the camera pans in at a close angle, it's hard not to notice if the performer is thirty years older than the character being played. These days there are certainly plenty of superb opera singers who also look like movie stars, and they're the ones most likely to appear on the big screen. A tepid staging like Grandage's for *Don Giovanni* can actually be more successful in the cinema than on stage—though it lacks a point of view, it also provides a blank canvas for the lead singers in the Live in HD performance. On a big screen, we can experience the charm and charisma of the Polish baritone Mariusz Kwiecień, Luca Pisaroni's winning Leporello, and the dynamic between the frustrated servant and his manipulative master up close. Fans of the superb German tenor Jonas Kaufmann were able to enjoy, via broadcasts, his much-lauded performance in the title role of Verdi's *Otello* at the Royal Opera in London. Although the broadcasts do not offer the thrill of hearing a singer live, they are a good (and inexpensive) alternative for those who can't make it to the theater. And unlike watching a DVD, experiencing opera at the cinema is a shared event, the closest thing to being at the opera house itself.

Traditionally, white singers portraying Otello (who, in the opera, as in Shakespeare's play, is described as a "Moor") have been "blacked up," even though such makeup has long been deemed offensive in the theater world. Keith Warner, who directed the production starring Kaufmann, said, "I've employed anybody of any color for any role all through my working life. I would never dream of asking a black singer to put on a white face, so why ask a white singer to black up? That's not the kind of theatre I'm interested in, and it's just not necessary: it's about the audience making an imaginative leap." In 2015, the Metropolitan Opera made the wise decision to stop using makeup to darken a singer's skin in *Otello*. Its production was directed by Bartlett Sher, who said at the time: "It really did seem very obvious given our cultural history and political history in the United States, that for me and my production team the idea of putting [Othello] in blackface was completely unthinkable." The director Francesca Zambello told the *New York Times* that year that if she were casting Otello, she "would work hard to find a black man who is vocally and dramatically appropriate for the role." If that wasn't possible, she "certainly would not present another singer 'blacked up.'" "The great stories and characters," she said, "fascinate us because we recognize something of ourselves—for better or for worse—in them, and not because of the color of their skin."

Color-blind casting is to be applauded, although directors are sometimes criticized for their decisions, as the Los Angeles Opera was when it cast Anthony Roth Costanzo (a superb white countertenor) in the title role of Philip Glass's *Akhnaten*, an Egyptian pharaoh. Two dozen demonstrators showed up on opening night in November 2016 with placards protesting the casting of a white performer in the role. "While we strive for overall diversity in our casting, we have a long-standing policy of ignoring age, race and other physical characteristics when it comes to casting particular roles," the opera company said in a statement.

Costanzo had previously sung the role in London; as the LA Opera noted at the time, he suited the role vocally and was able to fulfill the requirements for a production requiring physical agility and nuanced acting.

The derogatory expressions "park and bark" and "stand and shout" are often used to describe singers who mostly stand immobile, or limit themselves to stock gestures, as was common in the past. Joan Sutherland, who was often criticized for her lack of acting ability, said: "If you want to see a wonderful actress, you go to see a straight play," but singers are now expected to be convincing actors and actresses as well as good opera singers. Directors often ask them to carry out acrobatic moves or take uncomfortable postures while singing virtuosic music and projecting their voices. For his production of Wagner's *Lohengrin*, the director Robert Wilson asked the singers to move while enacting stylized poses that resembled *kabuki*, a type of Japanese dance-drama. Wilson was loudly booed at the premiere in 1998, but the production—an abstract staging featuring a haze of blue lighting—was more positively received at its revival in 2006. Wilson had relaxed the kabuki poses somewhat, although the singers still looked more uncomfortable than swanlike as they glided about the stage. However the audience may feel about avant-garde stagings, these kinds of approaches to opera can certainly prove hugely challenging to singers. The superb Finnish soprano Karita Mattila sang the role of Fiordiligi in an avant-garde production of Mozart's *Così fan tutte* at the Salzburg Festival in 2000 that included large insects as props. According to an interview with Mattila that year in the *New York*

Times, before singing "Come Scoglio" (Like a rock), the aria in which she asserts her fidelity, she entered the stage leading two men with a leash: they had to crawl like dogs, dressed in leathers and chains. "What was the point? There was none," she told the *Times*. "It was one of the worst experiences I've had for a long time. I didn't believe in the production. Nobody understood what they were doing or why. I've done many crazy things, but there is also a line one cannot cross." Some of the singers (including Mattila) who sang in Wilson's *Lohengrin* lamented the physical demands of the staging on the performers, who had to sing difficult roles while carrying out Wilson's extremely slow, stylized hand and arm movements.

It's worth noting that some productions that shock audiences at their premieres are much better received in the ensuing years, as Chéreau's Ring Cycle was at Bayreuth, and Wilson's *Lohengrin* at the Met. That's true for other kinds of art and music as well: pieces that seem shocking or disconcerting upon first viewing or listening gain acceptance once the audience becomes more familiar with them. The first time I saw Anthony Minghella's production of *Madama Butterfly* (which originated at the English National Opera in London), I was perplexed by the Bunraku puppet that was used to portray Butterfly's son—usually, the role is enacted by a little boy. Minghella had created a visually stunning panorama for the opera, with the onstage action reflected in an overhead mirror; I was distracted, however, by the three men in black who manipulated the puppet onstage. When I saw the production a few years later, the puppet seemed a reasonable and believable component of the opera. It's difficult to say why: it could have been because I was used to the puppet by then, or perhaps it was because the soprano interacted more naturally with the puppet. (Minghella, a film director, died in 2008.)

There is unquestionably an impractical element to seeing live opera—a five-hour work that finishes near midnight on a weekday clearly isn't ideal for people with long commutes, families, and day jobs. Theater directors sometimes trim works to make them more accessible to contemporary playgoers: a significant chunk of *Hamlet*, for example, is sometimes pruned. Scenes from Shakespeare's works are also sometimes rearranged: minor characters might be meshed into one, or unnecessary plot elements trimmed. The opera world is usually less flexible: when Patrice Chéreau asked the conductor Esa-Pekka Salonen whether he could rearrange a few scenes in Strauss's *Elektra*, for example, Salonen said, "Well, all hell would break loose." To which Chéreau replied, "You guys are killing yourselves in this classical world. Because if somebody would do the Sophocles text, nobody would ever expect to see anything but an arranged, newly created text—new translation, new dramaturgy, maybe even new material." Major opera houses in the United States tend to be cautious about making cuts or rearranging scenes; grassroots companies, such as Heartbeat Opera, have fewer qualms. In Europe, directors often push the envelope even further. A new production of *Carmen* that opened in Florence, Italy, in January 2018 ended with Carmen killing Don José, instead of the other way around: it was a symbolic gesture to illuminate the plight of the many Italian women murdered each year by jealous male partners.

There's still an element of formality at some major European opera houses, such as La Scala in Milan. An article in *The Telegraph* in July 2017 carried the headline "Italy's Elite La Scala Appalled at Opera Goers Turning Up in T-shirts, Mini-skirts and Flip-flops." The article noted that although the "worst culprits" were usually foreign tourists, even Italians were turning up in shorts and sandals. Ushers were reportedly sending inappropriately dressed ticket-holders to a nearby store to buy trousers or a dress. Some Italians have argued in favor of relaxing the dress code; others feel that it's important to respect the venue and other audience members by dressing elegantly. But La Scala is the only major opera house with an official dress code; at most traditional venues, people come dressed in everything from jeans to black tie attire. Jeans certainly predominate at the many off-the-beaten-track opera venues that have sprung up in recent years in North America and Europe, some of which are miles from the grand theaters associated with opera, not just in distance, but in attitude.

There are indie opera companies doing innovative work in many cities in both Europe and North America. In Italy, for example, OperaCamion is reaching new audiences by staging productions on a truck in outlying city neighborhoods. During performances of *Hopscotch*, a site-specific mobile opera in Los Angeles, audience members were serenaded in cars while being driven to various locations around the city. In Handel's era, patrons were seated according to both economic and social status, a hierarchy duplicated to some extent in traditional opera houses, because of the pricing for different tiers of seats. But it's often eliminated in off-the-beaten-track venues. Attending an opera in a small space or a cinema can be an alluring experience because you're close to the performers and the action—an intimacy that is inevitably missing at a performance in a vast space like the Metropolitan Opera, with its 3,800 seats—indeed, a large opera house can seem ill-suited for much of baroque and contemporary opera.

There's a trade-off in the cinema and at small indie theaters: in these venues, the audience cannot experience the power and precision of the world's great opera orchestras live, or bask in the sound of an extraordinary, unamplified voice in a large space. In the opera house, assuming there are good acoustics, the unamplified voices of the singers are democratically dispersed, even if some seats are closer than others and therefore superior in visual terms. Opera-goers can enjoy the singing—the most important element of opera—from any vantage point.

Debussy, during a youthful conversation in Paris in 1889 with his teacher, cryptically remarked that in opera "there is too much singing," but surely there's no such thing as too much singing. We're lucky to live in an era when we have so many opportunities to enjoy the operatic voice—on stage, at the cinema, on the radio, in unexpected locations, and around the clock via our ubiquitous gadgets.

EPILOGUE

While finishing the final draft of this book, I had perhaps the ultimate twenty-first-century opera experience. I watched *La bohème* on my computer, beamed live into my living room from the Paris Opera, courtesy of an online platform called Medici.tv. In this futuristic production, by the German director Claus Guth, the bohemians' garret was updated to a spaceship and the bohemians wore spacesuits. The singing was superb and the staging was often visually stunning. In the four hundred years since Monteverdi's Orfeo first descended to the underworld, opera has gone in all directions, including ascending to outer space in this Puccini production. Although speculating about what lies ahead can be as fruitless as wallowing in nostalgia, I feel confident in asserting that the future holds many riches for opera. We can't know whether in 2118 people will be watching opera on newfangled gadgets right here on earth, or while taking a vacation to a galaxy far, far away, but we do know that the current crop of singing actors is superb, the level of orchestral playing in major houses is high, composers are busy writing new works, small entrepreneurial companies are offering imaginative productions, and directors are thinking creatively about how to stage opera.

Despite the enormous difficulties of making a life in opera and the years of specialized training necessary, there is no shortage of young people who want to give it a shot—their talent is on display at prestigious competitions, artist-in-training programs, and smaller theaters. A language is in danger of extinction only when there are no longer any practitioners; in the same way, the challenge in opera is to prevent it from becoming an exclusive conversation between specialists. I hope this book will encourage nascent opera fans to explore all corners of the remarkable operatic repertory and help them understand how the many pieces of this all-encompassing art form fit together.

Some observers have wondered whether opera, with its artifice, is a good fit for the twenty-first century. But perhaps the unrealism of opera renders it the ultimate art form for this century—an era of Photoshopped images in which people idealize their personal lives for public consumption on social media. Our era, with its digital disguises, is an unnatural one on many levels. Yet despite its artificial elements, opera, with its un-airbrushed emotions, is also the antidote to artificiality: you're never unsure about what a character really feels. Opera—and the power of the human voice—provides the authentic and heart-wrenching catharsis so very much needed in our time.

ACKNOWLEDGMENTS

ACCORDING TO FAMILY ANECDOTE, I BEGGED FOR A PIANO at age six after hearing my great uncle, George Field, play. I am fortunate that my parents, Eluned and Julian Schweitzer, indulged this wish and nurtured my early love of music and the passion for writing that followed soon after. Music teachers in my formative years, including my chamber music teacher Oliver Edel and my piano teacher Thomas Schumacher, taught me how to really listen to the inner workings of a score.

Zoë Pagnamenta, my opera-loving agent, encouraged me to pitch this book, and the skill and enthusiasm of Brian Distelberg, my brilliant editor at Basic Books, helped shape the manuscript into a cohesive whole. Basic's production team, including Melissa Veronesi and copyeditor Kathy Streckfus, diligently guided the book through the final stages.

This book benefited enormously from the input of a number of people. The encyclopedic knowledge of David

Shengold, Paul Pelkonery and George Loomis, who all read drafts, proved invaluable. James Jacobs and Carlo Vutera read chapters and provided insightful suggestions. Allan Kozinn, Eluned and Julian Schweitzer, and Ada and Dina Brunstein also offered vital feedback.

Ellen Butters, a friend and chamber music partner, kindly designed my website. Marissa Jones, Anthony Gottlieb, Anthony Tommasini, Cynthia Rojas-Sejas, and Natasha Becker offered encouragement. I am also grateful to my brother, Gareth, for his constant support, and to Sarathi, for his love, patience, and willingness to venture into the world of opera.

NOTES

PREFACE

1   **"Chamber Pot Opera's Queen Victoria Building..."**: Nick Galvin, "Chamber Pot Opera's Queen Victoria Building Venue an Inconvenience for Some," *Sydney Morning Herald*, June 4, 2017.

3   **"people are wrong when they say..."**: Noël Coward, *Design for Living*, Act 3, scene 1, 1932.

6   **"is so visceral, so emotional..."**: Fiona Maddocks, "Antonio Pappano Interview: This Elitist Label Is Tiresome. Opera Is So Visceral," *The Guardian*, May 10, 2014.

CHAPTER 1

8   **"both poet and musician have depicted..."**: Thomas Kelly, *Five Nights: Five Musical Premieres* (New Haven, CT: Yale University Press, 2001), 56.

8   **"Whenever I go to an opera..."**: David Littlejohn, *The Ultimate Art: Essays Around and About Opera* (Berkeley: University of California Press, 1993), 3.

11   **"to delight the ear..."**: Michael Rose, *The Birth of an Opera: Fifteen Masterpieces from Poppea to Wozzeck* (New York: W. W. Norton, 2013), 2.

12 **"for the first time..."**: Ovid, *Metamorphoses*, Book X: 1–85, Ovid Collection, University of Virginia Electronic Text Center, http:ovid.lib.virginia.edu/trans/Metamorph10.htm.

18 **"The only thing I have to say about the difference..."**: New Music Box staff, "In Your Opinion, What Is the Difference Between Opera and Musical Theater?: Stephen Sondheim, Composer and Lyricist," New Music USA, April 1, 2001, https:nmbx.newmusicusa.org/In-your-opinion-what-is-the-difference-between-opera-and-musical-theater-Stephen-Sondheim-Composer-and-Lyricist.

36 **"I have to separate my mind from my body..." / "and what it consists of..."**: Alice Coote, "My Life as a Man," *The Guardian*, May 13, 2015.

37 **"Opera is hopefully a democratic process..."**: Vivien Schweitzer, "Male Roles? Yes, but Ready for Divadom," *New York Times*, March 29, 2013.

38 **"the ignorant vanity of singers"**: Rose, *Birth of an Opera*, 27.

39 **"Happy people!..."**: Matthew Boyden, *The Rough Guide to Opera*, 3rd ed. (London: Rough Guides, 2002), 78.

44 **"in an opera the poetry must absolutely be..."**: Rose, *Birth of an Opera*, 78.

44 **"wholly contrary to my temperament..."**: Joan Acocella, "Nights at the Opera: The Man Who Put Words to Mozart," *The New Yorker*, January 8, 2007.

46 **"thorny roses"**: Liner notes, Mozart, *Le Nozze di Figaro*, no translator credited, Silvio Varviso conducting the Royal Philharmonic Orchestra, recorded live at Glyndebourne on June 9, 1962, CD GFOCD 001-62.

52 **"country wenches..."**: Liner notes, *Don Giovanni*, Teodor Currentzis conducting MusicAeterna, recorded in Perm, Russia, from November 23 to December 7, 2015, CD Sony Classical, 88985316032.

CHAPTER 2

61 **"Opera, through singing..."**: Robert Levine, *Weep, Shudder, Die: A Guide to Loving Opera* (New York: HarperCollins, 2011), 127.

65   **"because they are intimidated…":** Lizzy Davies, "La Scala's New Boss Takes Aim at 'Crazy' Catcalling of the Loggionisti Opera Fans," *The Guardian*, March 20, 2014.

69   **"let herself be lulled by the melodies…":** Gustave Flaubert, *Madame Bovary*, translated by Alan Russell (New York: Penguin, 1950), 234.

76   **"Opera is just like tennis or boxing…":** Peter Conrad, "Vittorio Grigolo: 'Opera Is Just Like Boxing or Formula 1. It's Dangerous,'" *The Guardian*, September 10, 2011.

77   **"She sings and declaims…":** Philip Gossett, *Divas and Scholars: Performing Italian Opera* (Chicago: University of Chicago Press, 2006), 272.

79   **"she paid attention to the text…":** Vivien Schweitzer, "At the Met, a Soprano Ascendant," *New York Times*, April 19, 2011.

CHAPTER 3

83   **"Out of the clear blue ether…":** Ernest Newman, *The Wagner Operas*, rev. ed. (Princeton, NJ: Princeton University Press, 1991), 127.

90   **"a sane person…":** Jonathan Lieberson, "Bombing in Bayreuth," *New York Review of Books*, November 10, 1988.

91   **"It is the sincere and heartfelt yearning…":** Paul Thomason, essay in Metropolitan Opera program note about *Tristan and Isolde*, https:cdn.metopera.org/metoperafiles/season/2016-17/operas/tristan_und_isolde/programs/102716%20Tristan.pdf.

91   **"see and hear such crazy lovemaking…":** Ibid.

94   **"You can lose yourself in it…":** Nigel Farndale, "Antonio Pappano: 'I Haven't Time to Sit Through The Ring," *Daily Telegraph*, June 27, 2015.

97   **"It was the almost physical presence…":** Anthony Tommasini, "Nilsson in Person: The Glory of the Power," *New York Times*, January 14, 2006.

97   **"You had to have heard the voice live…":** Edward Seckerson, "It Don't Mean a Thing If It Ain't Got That Ping: The Legendary Birgit Nilsson Is in Town to Talk About Old Times

and Great Roles, from Wagner's Brunnhilde to Puccini's Turandot," *The Independent*, May 24, 1993.

101   **"altogether of people who are young…":** Emily Anderson, ed., *The Letters of Mozart and His Family*, 3rd ed. (Basingstoke, UK: Palgrave Macmillan, 1997).

105   **the most performed opera worldwide:** "Opera Statistics 2015/16," Operabase.com, www.operabase.com/top.cgi ?lang=en&splash=t.

109   **"My weapon is my tongue…":** Jessica M. MacMurray, ed., *The Book of 101 Opera Librettos: Complete Original Language Texts with English Translations* (New York: Black Dog and Leventhal, 1996).

111   **"If I could only make four characters…":** Charles Osborne, *The Opera Lovers' Companion* (New Haven, CT: Yale University Press, 2004), 498.

Chapter 4

118   **"Love is a rebellious bird…":** Jessica M. MacMurray, ed., *The Book of 101 Opera Librettos: Complete Original Language Texts with English Translations* (New York: Black Dog and Leventhal, 1996).

120   **"Here on the stage you shall behold…":** MacMurray, ed., *Book of 101 Opera Librettos*.

122   **Three of his operas:** "Opera Statistics 2015/16," Operabase. com, www.operabase.com/top.cgi?lang=en&splash=t.

122   **"sickened by the cheapness and emptiness":** Paul Kildea, ed., *Britten on Music* (New York: Oxford University Press, 2003), 30.

122   **"shabby little shocker":** Joseph Kerman, *Opera as Drama* (New York: Vintage, 1956), 254.

124   **"a millionaire in spirit":** MacMurray, ed., *Book of 101 Opera Librettos*.

125   **"a masterly piece of trash":** Michele Girardi, *Puccini: His International Art* (Chicago: University of Chicago Press, 2000), 190.

129   **"on the opera stage women…":** Catherine Clément, *Opera, or the Undoing of Women* (Minneapolis: University of Minnesota Press, 1979), 5.

129 **"Almost every time they started to speak..."**: Sheryl Sandberg and Adam Grant, "Speaking While Female," *New York Times*, January 12, 2015.

132 **"Light as a feather she flutters..."**: MacMurray, ed., *Book of 101 Opera Librettos*.

133 **"dear little woman..."**: Alexandra Wilson, *Opera: A Beginner's Guide* (London: Oneworld Publications, 2010), 126.

133 **"tip the scales a bit..." / "there's something fetishistic..."**: Mary Von Aue, "A Radical Redo for 'Madama Butterfly'—to Save It?," *New York Times*, May 19, 2017.

135 **"I would bind Jenůfa..."**: Liner notes, Leoš Janáček's *Jenůfa*, translated by Deryck Viney, Sir Charles Mackerras conducting the Vienna Philharmonic, recorded in Vienna, April 1982, CD Decca: 475 8227, p. 7.

136 **"All he sees in you..."**: Ibid.

140 **"My soul is sad!..."**: Liner notes, Mussorgsky's *Boris Godunov*, translated by David Lloyd-Jones, Herbert von Karajan conducting the Vienna Philharmonic, recorded in Vienna, November 1970, CD Decca: 475 7718.

CHAPTER 5

141 **"terribly cacophonous"**: Michele Girardi, *Puccini: His International Art* (Chicago: University of Chicago Press, 2000), 267.

142 **"...repugnant to Anglo-Saxon minds"**: "*Salome* in New York," *Musical News*, March 9, 1907, 32.

142 **"the drama of *Pelléas*..."**: Richard Langham Smith, "Pelléas et Mélisande," Grove Music Online, 2002, available at www.oxfordmusiconline.com/grovemusic/view/10.1093/gmo/9781561592630.001.0001/omo-9781561592630-e-5000002420.

144 **"body is hideous..."**: Jessica M. MacMurray, ed., *The Book of 101 Opera Librettos: Complete Original Language Texts with English Translations* (New York: Black Dog and Leventhal, 1996).

146 **"She is monstrous"**: Ibid.

147 **"When I, with eyes wide open, sleepless lie..."**: Liner notes, Richard Strauss, *Elektra*, no translator credited, Valery

Gergiev conducting the London Symphony Orchestra, recorded at the Barbican, London, January 11–14, 2010, CD LSO0701.

150 **"emancipation of the dissonance":** Richard Cohn, Brian Hyer, Carl Dahlhaus, Julian Anderson, and Charles Wilson, "Harmony," Grove Music Online, 2001, available at www .oxfordmusiconline.com/grovemusic/view/10.1093/gmo /9781561592630.001.0001/omo-9781561592630-e -0000050818?rskey=LS1hEZ&result=3.

150 **"dependent on people I hate…":** Alex Ross, *The Rest Is Noise: Listening to the 20th Century* (New York: Farrar, Straus and Giroux, 2007), 68.

151 **"capital offense":** Anthony Tommasini, *The New York Times Essential Library: Opera—A Critics' Guide to the 100 Most Important Works and the Best Recordings* (New York: Times Books / Henry Holt, 2004), 18.

154 **"listeners are stunned…":** Laurel Fay, "Lady Macbeth of the Mtsensk District," Grove Music Online, 2002, available at www.oxfordmusiconline.com/grovemusic/view/10.1093 /gmo/9781561592630.001.0001/omo-9781561592630-e -5000002507?rskey=I6reTy&result=1.

159 **"contrary to the requirements…":** Alexandra Ivanoff, "'Porgy and Bess' with a White Cast Stirs Controversy," *New York Times,* January 30, 2018.

159 **"When I first began work…":** George Gershwin, "Rhapsody in Catfish Row," *New York Times,* October 20, 1935.

160 **"a special brand of musical theater…":** Liner Notes, Original Cast Recording of *Street Scene,* Kurt Weill Foundation for Music, https:www.kwf.org/pages/wt-liner-notes-for-the -original-cast-recording-of-street-scene.html.

161 **"decorative, positive and charming":** *A Time There Was,* film about Benjamin Britten, directed by Tony Palmer, 1979.

162 **"the struggle of the individual…":** Philip Brett, *Music and Sexuality in Britten: Selected Essays* (Berkeley: University of California Press, 2006), 28.

164 **"His voice is like a long plaint…":** Jon Vickers, Tenor— Obituary, *The Telegraph,* July 12, 2015.

165 **"Who holds himself apart…":** Liner notes, Benjamin

Britten's *Peter Grimes*, Mark Wigglesworth conducting the
London Philharmonic Orchestra, recorded live at Glyndebourne in June, July, and August 2010, CD Glyndebourne
label: GFOCD 008-00.

170   **"Here's an end to your life as a rover..."**: Liner notes, Mozart, *The Marriage of Figaro*, David Parry conducting the
Philharmonia Orchestra, Jeremy Sams, trans., CD Chandos:
Opera in English, CHAN 3113(3).

171   **"I'm Papageno, that's my name..."**: Mozart, *The Magic Flute*,
2015–16 Metropolitan Opera Educator Guide, https:www
.metopera.org/metoperafiles/education/Educator%20Guides
/Ed%20Guide%20pdfs/Magic.Flute.guide.pdf.

173   **"an exotic and irrational entertainment..."**: Fred R. Shapiro and Joseph Epstein, eds., *The Yale Book of Quotations* (New
Haven, CT: Yale University Press, 2006).

174   **"There's the vowels, open words..."**: *Inside Opera: Why Does
It Matter?*, online course at futurelearn.com, Week 3, Part
3.7, Kings College, London, https:www.futurelearn.com
/courses/inside-opera.

CHAPTER 6

178   **589 operatic works:** *OPERA America: North American Opera
Report* (2015), www.nypublicradio.org/media/resources/2015
/Sep/16/OA_Mellon_2015.pdf.

178   **543 premieres worldwide:** "Opera Statistics 2015/16,"
Operabase.com, www.operabase.com/top.cgi?lang=en&splash=t.

180   **"We wanted to do a proscenium piece..."**: Mark Swed,
"Philip Glass' 'Einstein' Is Opera Because 'That's Where the
Stuff Was,'" *Los Angeles Times*, October 5, 2013.

181   **"usually reaches a point..."**: Richard Kostelanetz and Robert
Flemming, eds., *Writings on Glass: Essays, Interviews, Criticism*
(Berkeley: University of California Press, 1999), 172.

185   **"Respect women...." / "We live in an unsettled time..."**:
Liner notes, John Adams, *Nixon in China*, Marin Alsop conducting the Colorado Symphony Orchestra, Naxos American
Classics, recorded in Colorado, June 6–14, 2008, CD Naxos:
8.669022-24.

185   **"was a man who did have a heart..."**: Richard Scheinin, "John Adams on First—and Perhaps Favorite Opera, *Nixon in China*," *Mercury News*, June 7, 2012.

186   **"neither deify nor demonize..."**: Notes from librettist Mark Campbell, "The Evolution of (R)evolution," Santa Fe Opera 2017 season book, 80.

187   **"while the opera itself is not anti-Semitic..."**: "ADL Welcomes Metropolitan Opera's Decision to Cancel Global Simulcast of 'The Death of Klinghoffer,'" Anti-Defamation League press release, June 17, 2004, https:www.adl.org /news/press-releases/adl-welcomes-metropolitan-operas -decision-to-cancel-global-simulcast-of-the.

187   **"My father's house was razed...." / "They should have killed me..."**: Alice Goodman's libretto, Boosey and Hawkes, 1990, www.boosey.com/downloads/KlinghofferLibretto.pdf.

190   **"absence of will, of purpose"**: "Thomas Adès on What Inspired His New Opera *The Exterminating Angel*," Royal Opera House, May 2, 2017, www.roh.org.uk/news/thomas-ades -what-inspired-the-exterminating-angel.

192   **"I thought it's such a brilliant film..."**: AFP, "Opera Revisits Dark Dynamic in 'Breaking the Waves,'" *Daily Mail*, January 5, 2017.

193   **"It is ridiculous to prolong the sentence..."**: Bernard Williams, *On Opera* (New Haven, CT: Yale University Press, 2006), 7.

196   **"compressing the important events..."**: A. O. Scott, "Infidelity, Grandly Staged," *New York Times*, November 15, 2012.

203   **"If I'm really honest..."**: Justin Davidson, "Justin Davidson on Composer Mark-Anthony Turnage and His *Anna Nicole* Opera," Vulture, August 27, 2013, www.vulture.com/2013/08 /anna-nicole-smith-opera.html.

204   **"And there's no one to dress me..."**: Philip Hensher, *Powder Her Face*, Faber Music, 1995, http:web.mit.edu/jscheib /Public/phf/PowderHerFaceLibretto.pdf.

205   **"It is foolish to argue..."**: Kyle Gann, *Robert Ashley: American Composer* (Champaign: University of Illinois Press, 2012), 58.

206   **"I put my pieces in television format…"**: Kyle Gann, *Music Downtown: Writings from the Village Voice* (Berkeley: University of California Press, 2006), 20.

CHAPTER 7

210   **"I was scandalized that they were so scandalized"**: Daniel J. Wakin, "The Opera Goes to the Library, and the Talk Turns to (What Else?) 'Tosca'," *New York Times*, October 8, 2009.

211   **"simian creatures, hunched, hairy and horny…"**: Shirley Apthorp, "Rigoletto, Bavarian State Opera, Munich," *Financial Times*, February 24, 2005.

212   **"marvelous transformation scenes…"**: Evan Baker, *From the Score to the Stage: An Illustrated History of Continental Opera Production and Staging* (Chicago: University of Chicago Press, 2013), 11.

212   **"the two winged dragons…"**: Ibid., 2.

212   **"vast and motley crowd of citizens…"**: Helen M. Greenwald, essay in Metropolitan Opera program notes about *La bohème*, www.metopera.org/metoperafiles/season/2017-18 /operas/boheme/programs/022418Boheme.pdf.

220   **"I avoided interpretations"**: Anne Midgette, "Four Interpretations of Wagner's Ring Cycle," *Washington Post*, April 19, 2009.

222   **"Specifically now, what resonates…"**: Susan Galbraith, "Francesca Zambello on Directing The Ring of the Nibelung at WNO," DC Theater Scene, April 26, 2016, https: dctheatrescene.com/2016/04/26/francesca-zambello -directing-ring-nibelung-wno.

222   **"never encountered anything more false and foolish"**: *An Encyclopedia of Quotations About Music*, compiled and edited by Nat Shapiro (New York: Da Capo, 1981 [1978]), 245.

224   **"I've employed anybody of any color…"**: Warwick Thompson, "Verdi's Greatest Challenge? The Pressures and Delights of Tackling Otello," Royal Opera House, March 3, 2017, www .roh.org.uk/news/verdis-greatest-challenge-the-pressures -and-delights-of-tackling-otello.

225 **"It really did seem very obvious..."**: Nicky Woolf, "Decision to Scrap Blackface from Otello Not Complicated, Says Met Director," *The Guardian*, September 22, 2015.

225 **"would work hard to find a black man..."**: Michael Cooper, "An 'Otello' Without Blackface Highlights an Enduring Tradition in Opera," *New York Times*, September 15, 2015.

225 **"While we strive for overall diversity in our casting..."**: Catherine Womack, "Demonstrators Protest L.A. Opera over Casting of White Singer as an Egyptian Pharaoh," *Los Angeles Times*, November 6, 2016.

226 **"If you want to see a wonderful actress..."**: Susan Heller Anderson, "Joan Sutherland Returns to the Met in 'Lucia,'" *New York Times*, October 31, 1992.

227 **"What was the point?..."**: Anthony Tommasini, "A Soprano Takes a Spiritual Turn," *New York Times*, October 13, 2000.

228 **"Well, all hell would break loose" / "You guys are killing yourselves..."**: Michael Cooper, "Can You Shorten That Aria? Opera Weighs Cuts in the Classics," *New York Times*, July 6, 2016.

229 **"Italy's Elite La Scala Appalled..."**: Nick Squires, "Italy's Elite La Scala Appalled at Opera Goers Turning Up in T-shirts, Mini-skirts and Flip-flops," *The Telegraph*, July 14, 2007.

230 **"there is too much singing"**: Roger Nichols, *The Life of Debussy* (Cambridge: Cambridge University Press, 1998), 58.

RECOMMENDED RESOURCES
AND BIBLIOGRAPHY

There have never before been so many ways to explore opera, including via online platforms such as Spotify, YouTube, and iTunes. The websites of major opera companies, including the Royal Opera (roh.org) and the Metropolitan Opera (metopera.com), as well as of regional theaters, are often a great resource, supplying detailed synopses, program essays, artist interviews, and feature articles. The Met also offers radio broadcasts of Saturday matinee performances, live audio streams, and (for a subscription) access to its vast trove of recordings and Live in HD broadcasts. An informative online opera course is available at Future Learn (www.futurelearn.com /courses/inside-opera). The subscription-based platform Medici.tv features live streaming of operas (as well as concerts and ballets) and an extensive archive. Of course, if you live near an opera house, you should check out their offerings and buy a ticket! Opera tickets can be much more affordable than a typical Broadway musical. If you're not near any opera theaters, you may be able to enjoy a live broadcast at your local cinema. Many of the operas discussed in this book, including the new operas of Chapter 6 and the productions highlighted in Chapter 7, are available on DVD.

While researching this book I often consulted *Oxford Music Online*, a subscription-based portal to *The New Grove Dictionary of Opera*, a comprehensive, reliable, and frequently updated source of information about every component of opera. The library of a budding opera fan should include *The Grove Book of Operas*, a valuable reference book edited by Stanley Sadie and Laura Macy that features background information and detailed synopses for some 250 operas. For an engaging history with a focus on music before the contemporary era, I recommend Carolyn Abbate and Roger Parker's *A History of Opera* (New York: W. W. Norton, 2015), and for a vivid survey of twentieth-century classical music and opera, see Alex Ross's *The Rest Is Noise: Listening to the 20th Century* (New York: Farrar, Straus and Giroux, 2007). Anthony Tommasini's *The New York Times Essential Library: Opera—A Critics' Guide to the 100 Most Important Works and the Best Recordings* (New York: Times Books / Henry Holt, 2004) can help you build a library of important recordings. The coffee-table book *Opera: Passion, Power and Politics*, edited by Kate Bailey (London: V&A Publishing, 2017), was produced in conjunction with the exhibit of the same name at the Victoria and Albert Museum and offers insightful essays about seven important operas from the Renaissance to the twentieth century in the context of the cities and cultures in which they were created. In *The Inner Voice: The Making of a Singer*, the soprano Renée Fleming offers an insider's glimpse of the opera world as well as valuable insights into vocal technique and the mechanics of the operatic voice, the most hidden and elusive of instruments.

Abbate, Carolyn, and Roger Parker. *A History of Opera* (updated edition). New York: W. W. Norton, 2015.

Anderson, Emily, ed. *The Letters of Mozart and His Family*, 3rd ed. Basingstoke: Palgrave Macmillan, 1997.

Baker, Evan. *From the Score to the Stage: An Illustrated History of Continental Opera Production and Staging*. Chicago: University of Chicago Press, 2013.

Bock, Duncan, ed. *The Little Book of Opera*. New York: Balliett and Fitzgerald, 1996.

Boyden, Matthew. *The Rough Guide to Opera*, 3rd ed. London: Rough Guides, 2002.

Cairns, David. *Mozart and His Operas*. Berkeley: University of California Press, 2006.

Clément, Catherine. *Opera, or the Undoing of Women*. Minneapolis: University of Minnesota Press, 1979.

Gann, Kyle. *Music Downtown: Writings from the Village Voice*. Berkeley: University of California Press, 2006.

———. *Robert Ashley: American Composer*. Champaign: University of Illinois Press, 2012.

Girardi, Michele. *Puccini: His International Art*. Chicago: University of Chicago Press, 2000.

Gossett, Philip. *Divas and Scholars: Performing Italian Opera*. Chicago: University of Chicago Press, 2006.

Hines, Jerome. *Great Singers on Great Singing*. New York: Limelight, 1984.

Kelly, Thomas. *Five Nights: Five Musical Premieres*. New Haven, CT: Yale University Press, 2001.

Kerman, Joseph. *Opera as Drama*. New York: Vintage, 1956.

Kildea, Paul, ed. *Britten on Music*. New York: Oxford University Press, 2003.

Kostelanetz, Richard, and Robert Flemming. *Writings on Glass: Essays, Interviews, Criticism*. Berkeley: University of California Press, 1999.

Latham, Alison, ed. *The Oxford Companion to Music*. Oxford: Oxford University Press, 2002.

Levin, David J. *Unsettling Opera: Staging Mozart, Verdi, Wagner and Zemlinsky*. Chicago: University of Chicago Press, 2007.

Levine, Robert. *Weep, Shudder, Die: A Guide to Loving Opera*. New York: HarperCollins, 2011.

Littlejohn, David. *The Ultimate Art: Essays Around and About Opera*. Berkeley: University of California Press, 1993.

MacMurray, Jessica M., ed. *The Book of 101 Opera Librettos*. New York: Black Dog and Leventhal, 1996.

Magee, Brian. *The Tristan Chord: Wagner and Philosophy*. New York: Henry Holt, 2000.

McClatchy, J. D. *Seven Mozart Librettos: A Verse Translation*. New York: W. W. Norton, 2011.

Newman, Ernest. *The Wagner Operas*, rev. ed. Princeton, NJ: Princeton University Press, 1991.

Nichols, Roger. *The Life of Debussy*. Cambridge: Cambridge University Press, 1998.

Noonan, Ellen. *The Strange Career of Porgy and Bess: Race, Culture, and America's Most Famous Opera*. Chapel Hill: University of North Carolina Press, 2012.

Osborne, Charles. *The Opera Lovers' Companion*. New Haven, CT: Yale University Press, 2004.

Plotkin, Fred. *Opera 101: A Complete Guide to Learning and Loving Opera*. New York: Hyperion, 1994.

Powell, Neil. *Benjamin Britten: A Life for Music*. New York: Henry Holt, 2013.

Rose, Michael. *The Birth of an Opera: Fifteen Masterpieces from Poppea to Wozzeck*. New York: W. W. Norton, 2013.

Ross, Alex. *The Rest Is Noise: Listening to the 20th Century*. New York: Farrar, Straus and Giroux, 2007.

Spencer, Stewart, and Barry Millington, eds. *Wagner's Ring of the Nibelung: A Companion*. New York: Thames and Hudson, 2013.

Swafford, Jan. *Language of the Spirit: An Introduction to Classical Music*. New York: Basic Books, 2017.

Tommasini, Anthony. *The New York Times Essential Library: Opera—A Critics' Guide to the 100 Most Important Works and the Best Recordings*. New York: Times Books / Henry Holt, 2004.

Wagner, Richard. *Opera and Drama*. Translated by Ashton Ellis. Lincoln: University of Nebraska Press, 1995.

Wagner, Richard. *The Ring of the Nibelung*. Translated by Andrew Porter. New York: W. W. Norton, 1976.

Williams, Bernard. *On Opera*. New Haven, CT: Yale University Press, 2006.

Wilson, Alexandra. *Opera: A Beginner's Guide*. London: Oneworld Publications, 2010.

INDEX

Credit: Chevas Rolfe

VIVIEN SCHWEITZER IS A writer and pianist based in New York. She worked for ten years as a classical music and opera critic for the *New York Times*. She has also written for the BBC, the *Moscow Times*, and *The Economist*.